To Don

3 Cheers for decision!

from Adèle

Christmas 1981

VINTAGE
NANTUCKET

BOOKS BY A.B.C. WHIPPLE

Vintage Nantucket
The Fatal Gift of Beauty:
     The Final Years of Byron and Shelley
Tall Ships and Great Captains
Pirate: Rascals of the Spanish Main
Yankee Whalers in the South Seas

For Younger Readers
The Mysterious Voyage of Captain Kidd
Hero of Trafalgar
Famous Pirates of the New World

VINTAGE
NANTUCKET

A.B.C.Whipple

Illustrated by Richard M. Powers

DODD, MEAD & COMPANY, New York

1 2 3 4 5 6 7 8 9 10

Library of Congress Cataloging in Publication Data

Whipple, Addison Beacher Colvin, date
Vintage Nantucket.

Includes index.
1. Nantucket, Mass.—History. 2. Nantucket, Mass.—
Description and travel. I. Title.
F72.N2W46   974.4'97   78-7107
ISBN 0-396-07517-7

This one is for MELISSA

FOREWORD

My wife and I first heard of Nantucket when we were
city apartment dwellers and a friend told us about the
island's empty beaches, open moors and friendly fauna.
There was an old schooner, she said, on whose deck you
could have lunch and feed the sea gulls. That did it. Off
we went to Nantucket for our wedding anniversary.

That was thirty-five years ago. In those days you could
travel from New York to Nantucket in luxury. The Night

Cape Codder's sleeping cars rolled out onto a pier from which you could step onto a ship that had wooden steamer chairs on deck and private staterooms below.

Perhaps it was because we were car-free, carefree urbanites that we discovered the extra attraction of Nantucket. For the first few years our explorations of the island were bounded by the distances we could cover on a bicycle, and thus we found Nantucket town to be a fascination unto itself. Other coastal and island resorts have beautiful beaches and lovely landscapes. But no other summer resort seems to have that extra element in such rich profusion as Nantucket does. The element, of course, is history. Every town has its history. But few we have visited can boast of quite such a colorful mixture as Nantucket has.

We walked through the living museum of the town. We read the accounts of the heroic, eccentric and independent people who inhabited the island. We marveled at the brave, not to say foolhardy, enterprise that made this hillock in the sea the capital of a thriving whaling industry. And we realized what Nantucketers mean when they say that there is something different about the island. It may be, as Nathaniel Benchley says, "a state of mind." To many it is an addiction. Most of this special attraction, to us at least, has come from the knowledge that we walk in the footsteps of so many fascinating Nantucketers.

Since this first discovery Nantucket has been a major part of our life. It has influenced the upbringing of two dogs, two children and innumerable friends of our children. We have stayed in hotels and inns, in cottages and houses at Surfside and Pocomo, in a boathouse on Old North Wharf and—our nostal-

gic favorite—a one-room cabin that had been a cob-
bler's shop, at the end of Fair Street; it was rented to
us by two incomparably hospitable Nantucket ladies,
the Misses Marie and Clementine Platt. So it seemed
only fitting when my publisher friend Phelps Platt,
though no relation to our late guardian angels, asked
me to write a history of Nantucket.

Hundreds of others have written about Nantucket's
history, from the first diarists to the historians of the
present day. I am of course indebted to all of them, but
most particularly to Nantucket's preeminent historian,
Edouard A. Stackpole. Former President of the Nantucket Historical Association and now Curator of the
Foulger Museum, Edouard Stackpole is, in my opinion,
the Samuel Eliot Morison of Nantucket; his *The Sea Hunters* is the classic book on whaling and sealing. And anyone interested in the island's heritage is deeply in Ed
Stackpole's debt.

His name is everywhere on the pages of a most useful
guide to Nantucket's history, a "bibliography of source
material" as its compiler, Marie M. Coffin, calls it. Its title
is *The History of Nantucket.* It was published in 1970 and
is the essential first book for anyone who wants to learn
more about the island's history. There also are special
sections of books on Nantucket in the town library, the
Atheneum (to the left of the main desk at this writing);
and there are special Nantucket shelves or sections in
most of the bookstores.

I have mentioned most of my favorites in the appropriate places in this book. But there are dozens of other
good volumes on Nantucket and its history, enough to
get you through at least a week of bad weather. As interesting as most of the books are the thousands of articles

in the *Proceedings* of the Nantucket Historical Association, and the Association's quarterly, *Historic Nantucket,* conveniently bound and indexed in the Foulger Museum.

Many friends as well as books helped me. Ed Stackpole read the manuscript, corrected some errors and gently guided me away from misstatements and misinterpretations; I take the responsibility, of course, for everything, including whatever he may have been too polite to point out. Adam ("Bud") Craig helped bring alive again that incredible business of whaling. Mrs. Elizabeth Little has done some important new research on Nantucket's Indians; you can find much of it in the *Proceedings* of the Historical Association. (And don't miss the paperback *The Nantucket Indians,* by Meredith Marshall Brenizer.) Mrs. Louise Hussey, Librarian at the Foulger Museum, was especially helpful. And Mrs. Lucile Bell, who lived in the Hadwen-Satler House as a bride, was full of fascinating information about Nantucket's recent years. Roy Larsen mentioned sources I might not otherwise have discovered. Joan Mebane led me to material on Siasconset. Clifford and Henna O'Hara's house at Pocomo has been the base for many of our excursions around the island. Not least am I indebted to our daughter Ann Marr for typing an almost illegible manuscript, and to my wife Jane, who contributed so much research and editorial advice (not to mention the index) that she should more properly be credited as coauthor.

A.B.C. Whipple
Old Greenwich,
Connecticut

CONTENTS

VINTAGE NANTUCKET

Figurehead from whaling ship

O<small>N</small> a September evening, under a waning moon, my wife and I went for a walk through the heart of Nantucket. The town was still. Our footsteps echoed down the long cavern of India Street. There was a soft sheen on the shingled houses, and the polished brass doorknockers reflected the light of the street lamps. The alleys of sky above the narrow streets were bright with

2

1
AN EVENING WITH NANTUCKET'S GHOSTS

stars in the clear island air.

It was a good time to explore Nantucket town. The daytime traffic was gone. Through the lighted windows we could see paneled hearths built centuries ago. Even more than in the light of day, we could sense all around us Nantucket's ages of history. It is in the evening that Nantucket's ghosts walk with you.

And it is a setting made for ghosts. Nowhere else in America are there so many houses of the 18th and early 19th centuries. There are at least four hundred of them, virtually unchanged. They are not reconstructions but originals. Williamsburg, Virginia, can show you what America's past must have been like; Nantucket shows you what it actually was.

We had prepared for our evening walk by studying the charming and informative book *Nantucket Doorways,* by the island's foremost historian, Edouard A. Stackpole. The section of town we chose had not only survived for more than two hundred years, it had also escaped a double threat of fire and progress. In 1846 a conflagration still known as The Great Fire leveled one-third of the town; we shall see that fire in Chapter X. A combination of circumstances spared these mellow old houses from the flames. Then, while other communities grew and defiled the landscape with Victorian and turn-of-the-century monstrosities, Nantucket was enduring a depression so severe that virtually nothing new was built in the town, especially this part of town. As we walked down India Street, along Centre Street and up Main Street, we were thankful that this compact area of houses had been spared more than any similar section in the U.S. It is an architectural time capsule. Shelley in Pompeii wrote that he stood "within the City disinterred." We stood in a city as unchanged as Pompeii, and never interred.

The houses along India Street were typical and evocative. It had been a street of whaling captains, and their houses showed it—tidy and ship-shape, lined up close to the street like rows of vessels at a wharf. Many of their entrances are double gangways, with two sets of steps leading to the landing stage at the doorway. (It is said that these were called "welcome stairways," indicating that you were welcome from either direction.) On a moonlit night like this there was a further illusion: some of the houses seemed almost like ships heeling to the wind. In fact, they are off-center, with two sets of windows on one side of the doorway and one set on the other. And along the sidewalk in front of these homes the picket fences are topped by a ship's rail, for a better hand-hold in wet and windy weather.

These houses also reflected something else: the Quaker tradition. Nantucket was at once the whaling capital of the world and a center for the Society of Friends. The Quakers believed in practical simplicity. Practical and simple their houses are, and attractive as only functional beauty can be. The Quakers did not intend it—beauty for its own sake was to them an abomination—but they left us a heritage of loveliness in these narrow streets of Nantucket.

Their plain living nevertheless recalled to me a ditty of a peddler who once went from door to door in India Street, trying in vain to sell some of his goods to the parsimonious captains' wives. Finally he coined a despairing couplet:

Some folks call it Injy Street;
But *I* calls it stingy street.

Many of those thrifty captains' wives were shrewd busi-
nesswomen as well. At the foot of India Street we turned
right on Centre Street, to walk toward the town square,
and I imagined the busy scene it must have been during
Nantucket's heyday. Centre Street was lined with shops
and stores, nearly all managed by women whose husbands were far away in the Pacific Ocean pursuing the
sperm whale. So many of the shops were run by women
that Centre Street was known as Petticoat Row. The
wooden buildings were all burned by Nantucket's Great
Fire, and the old architecture of the town stops abruptly
here; this was the western limit of the fire. Centre Street
is again a row of shops, and tonight it was not difficult
to visualize those purposeful women in their long skirts
striding briskly to the bank at the corner. Good, gray,
ghostly women, managing the island's business while
their husbands were at sea, going up and down the
sweeping steps of the bank. The Pacific Bank, of course;
not the National Bank or the Nantucket Bank. The Pacific
was where the money came from. And the Pacific Bank
was where it was easy to summon up another ghost. She
lived in the bank.

Her name was Maria Mitchell. Her father was cashier
of the Pacific Bank; his family lived in an apartment in the
bank. And on the roof was a small observatory, through
whose telescope his daughter discovered in 1847 a
comet that made her world-famous. We will meet her in
Chapter VIII; but on this evening on Nantucket's nearly
deserted street I could all but see the tall figure of Maria

Mitchell coming down those steps and walking around the corner to Main Street.

Here again we were at a dividing line: The Great Fire roared up the square below us and threatened to sweep along Main Street to demolish Nantucket's most beautiful houses. Just above the Pacific Bank, at No. 72 Main Street, we could sense the presence of another island heroine. With the fire approaching the head of the square, Mrs. Lydia Barrett was asked to evacuate her big white house at 72 Main Street; the fire marshals were desperately trying to contain the conflagration, and were blowing up some houses in its path. Lydia Barrett announced that if they blew up her house they would blow her up with it. The fire marshals retreated—and so did the fire.

We keenly realized this providential change in the fire's direction as we walked up this magnificent thoroughfare. Once called State Street, then changed to Main Street, it is truly the glory of Nantucket. Coming to Main Street from India Street is like entering another world. Here in a few blocks we could see two discrete ages of Nantucket. No. 81 Main Street, for example, was the simple clapboard home of Captain Christopher Burdick. Beyond were the pride of Nantucket town: three brick mansions and two white-pillared Greek Revival masterpieces across the street. The contrast perfectly reflected the owners of these homes.

Captain Burdick was master of the sealing ship *Huntress;* I could imagine him clumping up Main Street to No. 81, as he did on an evening in June 1821, carrying his logbook in his calloused hand. His sea chest would be brought up by the crew, but only Captain Burdick carried the ship's log. Not until nearly a century and a half later would the rest of the world learn the importance of the log. Captain Burdick put it away and went to sea again. Ten years later, off the coast of Central America, he died of tropical fever; this time he was brought up Main Street in a cask. He was buried in Prospect Hill Cemetery and his secret was buried with him.

In the mid-20th century historian Edouard Stackpole came upon Christopher Burdick's log and found that the taciturn sealing skipper had sailed four hundred miles south of Cape Horn and had sighted a landmass that, as he recorded in the log, he "supposed to be a continent," years before explorers confirmed his discovery and charted the continent of Antarctica.

Up Main Street, beyond the plain home of the sealing captain, was a striking contrast. Here were the famous "Three Bricks," the graceful and luxurious houses built for three Starbuck brothers. Across from them were the porticoed mansions built for William Hadwen. The ghosts we could visualize here were almost flamboyant. The houses comprised a family compound—the Starbuck brothers on one side of the street and their sister Eunice, married to William Hadwen, on the other. Two more sisters and their husbands lived in houses next door.

The patriarch of the clan was Joseph Starbuck, who made millions with his whaleships. The relative value of a million dollars in the mid-19th century can be judged by the fact that all three brick mansions cost a total of $54,000. Joseph ordered the houses built for his sons, but cannily kept the title to all of them, just to make sure his sons would remain in the family business.

George, Matthew, William and their wives and children visited with the Starbuck daughters, Mary Swain (at No. 92) and Eliza Barney (at No. 100), and traipsed across Main Street to have tea with their Hadwen relatives. William and Eunice lived in one of the Greek Revival houses; emulating his father-in-law, Hadwen had the other house built for his adopted daughter. An added attraction was an upstairs ballroom with a ceiling that opened to the stars and a suspension floor to cushion the dancers' feet—and also protect the ceiling below it. Hadwen was as canny as Starbuck: he made his fortune not only by investing in whaleships but also in a candle factory where he made smokeless tapers that brought premium prices all over America and Europe.

A far cry from the simplicity of the 18th-century Quakers; we will look at this transformation in Chapters VIII and IX. Not far from the Starbuck-Hadwen compound, at the corner of Main Street, was No. 1 Pleasant Street. The tall French windows were alight as we rounded the corner, and we could imagine the festivities for which this house was famous. It was built in 1837 for a prosperous young whaling merchant, William Crosby, and his bride Elizabeth, daughter of the prominent whaling captain Seth Pinkham. The Crosby house quickly became a social center for the newly liberated Nantucketers, and the whole town, especially the Quakers, talked when one Crosby party introduced frozen mousse to the island. Few of the guests could disguise their envy as they admired the mansion's double drawing room, the hand-blocked wallpaper, the silver doorknobs and, in the east room, the first Chickering piano to be imported to the island.

As we walked past No. 1 Pleasant Street and looked in at a glittering chandelier, I could also imagine the secret, sanctimonious pleasure of some Nantucket Quakers when only a year after the house was built William Crosby lost nearly all his new fortune. In 1838 a fire swept the wharf where he had a huge amount of whale oil stored. He had barely recovered when The Great Fire of 1846 destroyed nearly all the rest of his holdings. The house at 1 Pleasant Street was sold, and the Crosby banquets and balls were no more. Fortunes fluctuated for Nantucket's whaling merchants, few more so than for William Crosby.

Pleasant Street was more aptly named for a Nantucketer who lived across the way and a few doors up from No. 1. He was Walter Folger, and his house at No. 8 Pleasant Street must still, on a night like this, echo with the ghostly tolling of a magnificent grandfather clock. Perhaps the most remarkable clock ever constructed, and certainly a wonder of its time, Walter Folger's invention not only indicated the seconds, minutes and hours of the day, as well as the days of the month, but also showed the phases of the moon, the positions of the sun and the height of the tide in Nantucket Harbor. The clock, built in 1790 and still working smoothly, can be seen in the Foulger Museum on Broad Street. Here on Pleasant Street we could almost sense the electrifying presence of the man regarded as the island genius: inventor, lawyer, teacher, historian and Nantucket's representative in Washington from 1817 to 1821. Educated only in the island's schools, Walter Folger taught himself higher mathematics and medicine, and during a diphtheria epidemic on the island he treated two doctors among his patients. He learned French in order to study the European philosophers and scientists; he learned astronomy from a French treatise on the subject brought to the island by a shipwrecked French sailor.

Nearly as remarkable as Walter Folger's clock was his telescope, the finest in the country, through which he discovered spots on Venus that professional astronomers had missed. One of the few successful nonwhaling business ventures on Nantucket was the factory that Folger built for spinning and weaving cotton and wool, to provide clothing and employment for his fellow islanders during the War of 1812. Standing in front of the simple shingled house at No. 8 Pleasant Street, we could imagine the old man, stocky and authoritative like his cousin Ben Franklin, walking briskly along his picket fence, his wispy hair and his floppy coat blowing in the breeze; he used to brag that every stitch of clothing he wore had been made on his looms.

Walter Folger outlived his looms, because whaling revived after the war, providing work for all and money to import clothes and anything else the Nantucketers needed. Whaling provided a fortune too for the man whose house we were now approaching. It is still called "Moor's End," as it was when Jared Coffin had it built in 1827, at what was then the edge of town. At the corner of Pleasant and Mill Streets we stood and admired the handsome brick facade, the fan over the doorway and the brick stoop with its iron railing. It was difficult to imagine anyone disliking such gracious living. But one person did: Mrs. Coffin.

The story is that she complained about being too far away from the social center of things. No doubt Jared

Coffin's foul-smelling tryworks next door had something to do with it. In any case, he was as good a provider as any wife would want. He obligingly built another mansion in the center of town, which is still known as the Jared Coffin House, on the corner of Centre and Broad Streets. It could also be called the "Fourth Brick," so closely does it resemble the Starbuck mansions on Main Street; the major difference is an added story.

But evidently it was not Moor's End that bothered Mrs. Coffin as much as Nantucket itself. The new house on Broad Street had scarcely been built when the Jared Coffins moved to Boston. Standing here on Pleasant Street and enjoying the beauty of Moor's End, I remarked on feminine ingratitude—and my wife remarked on the possible prejudice of male historians.

The three-quarter moon was higher now, silhouetting the balustraded platforms atop some of the houses. In such a light we could almost make out a gray-skirted figure on one of these housetop walks. I remember the first time I made the error of referring to a "widow's walk" in the presence of a Nantucketer; that terminology may be used on the mainland or on Martha's Vineyard, but on Nantucket it is simply a "walk." As my Nantucket friend explained, "A widow wouldn't have much use for one anymore."

Our route took us across High Street to Pine Street, past another Starbuck house, but quite a different one and of quite a different vintage. Here was a rare reminder of Nantucket's earliest days. In the 17th century the islanders lived in a cluster of houses on the shores of a small bay to the west of the town we were now walking through. This early settlement, which we will visit in

Chapter IV, was abandoned at the turn of the 18th century when the bay became landlocked; it is now known as Capaum Pond. The islanders moved east to the present town, bringing their houses with them—or the wood from their houses, to be more precise; so scarce was wood on the island even then that not a stick was left behind.

Most of the houses were rebuilt in different forms, but one was reconstructed virtually as it had been at the first settlement. There it had been known as Parliament House, because it had been the gathering place of most of the townspeople—all because of a dominating figure the settlers called the "Great Lady." She was Mary Starbuck, adviser to nearly everyone and one of the founders of Nantucket's Quaker church. When the Society of Friends met at Mary Starbuck's house, the overflow was so great that benches and chairs were set up in the front yard. Not in the present town, because there is no front yard; like most other houses in Nantucket town, the Starbuck house crowds up to the sidewalk. Standing in front of the house, at the corner of Pine and Summer Streets, we could visualize the Great Lady, holding the white railing as she descended the steps and graciously acknowledged the bows of her neighbors as she proceeded grandly down Pine Street toward the square.

To get there she might have gone down a narrow passage now known as Mooers' Lane, named for a Captain Mooers and not because it was a cowpath. At least that is the route we took, past a small house that must still be inhabited by two of the liveliest ghosts on Nantucket. The plain, attractive, shingled house at 7 Mooers' Lane was the home of Reuben Chase, a trusted lieuten-

ant of John Paul Jones during the American Revolution,
and Reuben's even more indomitable sister Deborah
Chase, who was said to weigh 350 pounds and was more
than a match for any man on the island; we will meet her
in Chapter VIII.

Here on Pine Street, Mooers' Lane and Fair Street,
which we were approaching, the older, simple and utilitarian houses predominated, only a block from the mansions of Main Street and Pleasant Street. Plain but comfortable houses, many of them provided by whaling
captains who could spend little time in them. Houses
that beckoned them home, and remained unchanging,
durable symbols of the stability they hoped to return to.
Some did. Captain Benjamin Worth sailed 870,000 miles
in forty-one years at sea, rounding Cape Horn sixteen
times and bringing home 19,000 barrels of whale oil
without losing a man, then retired and received the news
that his son, also a captain, had been killed in the Pacific
while attacking a whale.

On Fair Street we could see the house of Captain Seth
Pinkham. After a series of prosperous voyages, Captain
Pinkham retired to this house at 40 Fair Street. Then
came the depression of 1837; Captain Pinkham lost most
of his retirement investments. Next year a fire wiped out
his son-in-law, William Crosby of No. 1 Pleasant Street.
In 1840 Captain Pinkham went back to the Pacific. He
died at Pernanbuco, and his crew brought him home in
a pickle cask. They also brought home a full ship, which
provided for Captain Pinkham's family despite his death.

As we came down Fair Street to Main Street, I remembered Edouard Stackpole's account of a rainy day in the
mid-19th century and a curtained carriage rattling over

the cobblestones on its way up Main Street to a house at the corner of Prospect and Milk Streets. Two ship captains got out of the carriage and walked to the door of the house. Inside, Mrs. Samuel Joy said to her two sons: "I know what they are going to tell me. Thy father has been lost." Captain Joy's ship had sunk in the Pacific. Both of his sons became captains. And once again Mrs. Joy received the dreaded news: one of her sons had died of yellow fever in Hong Kong Harbor.

Near the corner of Fair and Main Streets was the former home of Captain John Macy, perhaps better known off the island today for his son, who tried shopkeeping and then whaling. A few months on a whaleship made shopkeeping seem more attractive, and the young man went to New York, where he opened a store under his own name: Rowland Hussey Macy.

By now the square was nearly empty. A lone automobile rumbled slowly, almost painfully, over the cobblestones. How the iron-bound wagon wheels must have resounded on those stones. No wonder they had curfew at 9 P.M. The cobblestones were brought to Nantucket as ships' ballast, and whatever discomfort they caused was preferable to the mud wallow that served as Nantucket's square before they were laid down. The stones were later extended to upper Main Street. Now, in the age of cement and macadam roads, why do they remain, forcing drivers to creep up the square and the street? Probably for just that reason. No one in his right mind would speed over this obstacle course; and if he did, his next stop would be at the garage or wheel alignment shop. Thus Nantucket grudgingly compromises with modern times: cars are permitted on Main Street, but only at the pace of last century's wagons and carts.

We turned down Centre Street again, stopping only to look at the pale moonlight on a lawn and garden at the corner of India Street. There was a late summer scent of flowers in the night air—and another lingering presence, of a remarkable woman who once lived here. Where now a lawn was bathed in moonlight once stood the home and shop of Kezia Coffin, the proudest and shrewdest of the matriarchy of Petticoat Row and one of the most famous and infamous women in Nantucket's history; we will meet her in Chapter VIII.

The pure-toned bell in the Unitarian Church tower began its toll. Curfew—no longer a law, but a gentle suggestion that reasonable people should be heading home. Still, one ghostly reminder remained.

At the corner of Centre and Broad Streets we could see two of Nantucket's most attractive old houses: the Jared Coffin mansion from which Mrs. Coffin fled to Boston, and a gift shop that had once been the home of Captain George Pollard.

I suppose it could be said of George Pollard that he was almost a ghost before his death. He was captain of the famous whaleship *Essex* that was stove in and sunk by a whale in 1820. Captain Pollard and his crew drifted across the Pacific in open whaleboats for nearly three months. Of the original twenty men only eight survived, and they did so by living off the flesh of their shipmates.

It was the story of the *Essex* that inspired Herman Melville to write his classic *Moby Dick*, pitting the great rogue whale against the megalomaniac Captain Ahab. On a foggy night in 1851, a year after the publication of his novel, Melville was in Nantucket on his first visit to the island. Like us, he was walking down Centre Street to the Jared Coffin House, then known as the Ocean House. As Melville and an islander passed the Pollard house, the old captain came down his steps.

Pollard had returned to sea after the tragedy of the *Essex,* only to be shipwrecked and rescued once more. He never sailed again. By 1851 he was one of the island's night watchmen. He raised his watchman's lantern as he went down the steps. In the swirling fog Melville caught a momentary glimpse of the old man's face by the light of the lantern. "Who is that man?" he asked his companion. Only then did the novelist realize that he was seeing the original of his immortal Captain Ahab. A ghost had come to life for Melville, as so many Nantucketers come to life for us whenever we mortals walk their streets.

ALTHOUGH Herman Melville did not visit Nantucket until after he had written *Moby Dick,* his description of the island is quoted by nearly everyone else writing about Nantucket. Far be it from me to break with so hallowed a tradition. Besides, what better place to start our study of Nantucket than on its map. And the story behind the creation of the island itself is as fascinating as the history made on it by its people. Melville wrote:

18

2
THE ISLAND

Great Point

Coskata

the Haulover

Wauwinet

Sesacacha Pond

Sankaty Head

Coatue

Pocomo

Polpis

Quidnet

Quasi

Shawkemo Hills

Altar Rock

Siasconset

Miacomet Pond

Surfside

Tom Nevers Head

Take out your map and look at it. See what a real corner of
the world it occupies; how it stands there away off shore, more
lonely than the Eddystone Lighthouse. Look at it—a mere
hillock, an elbow of sand; all beach, without a background.
There is more sand there than you would use in twenty years
as a substitute for blotting paper. Some gamesome wights will
tell you that they have to plant weeds there, they don't grow
naturally: that they import Canada thistles; that they have to
send beyond the seas for a spile to stop a leak in an oil cask;
that pieces of wood in Nantucket are carried about like bits of
the true cross in Rome; that people there plant toadstools
before their houses, to get under the shade in summertime;
that one blade of grass makes an oasis, three blades in a day's
walk a prairie; that they wear quicksand shoes, something like
Laplander snow-shoes; that they are so shut up, belted about,
every way inclosed, surrounded, and made an utter island of
by the ocean, that to their very chairs and tables small clams
will sometimes be found adhering, as to the backs of sea tur-
tles. But these extravaganzas only show that Nantucket is no
Illinois.

Illinois it certainly is not. An accident of nature it is.
One of Nantucket's legends concerns a Cape Cod Indian
giant named Maushop whose sleep was disturbed by
sand in his moccasins. Kicking fitfully, Maushop sent his
moccasins flying through the air. One landed nearby and
became the island of Martha's Vineyard. The other
sailed farther out to sea and became Nantucket. The fact
is that this is almost literally how the islands were born.
The only difference is that it was not a giant Indian but
an even more gigantic creator: a glacier.

Millions of years ago the land that now lies buried
more than 700 feet below Nantucket was part of a vast,
sloping coastal plain, stretching away to the ocean 100

miles or more to the east. Dinosaurs roamed through its towering forests. But the oceans rose and invaded the land over and over again, each time drowning the forests, driving the prehistoric creatures away or drowning them, and depositing layers of mud on the landscape. The dinosaurs disappeared, to be replaced by camels and horses that grazed on the marshy plains.

Then, about 600,000 years ago, came the Pleistocene Epoch, the time of the ice ages; four times the climate gradually grew colder. Snow and ice formed into glaciers in what is now Greenland and northern Canada, and the great sheets of ice moved south. For tens of thousands of years they ground over the land, at the rate of about 150 feet per year, compressing it under the weight of a mile-high mass of ice and moving much of the land's surface layer along with them.

Geologist Sidney Horenstein calls a glacier "at once a bulldozer, a file and a sled." As the glaciers moved over the land they chiseled and etched it, rounded and smoothed it. They dug out enormous chunks of soil, gravel and rock, churning it and grinding it into bits and pieces. Gravel became sand. Boulders big enough to survive were split and chipped. And the detritus was carried many miles south.

Finally the glaciers reached the southern, more temperate latitudes. And gradually the global climate warmed again. The glaciers retreated—melting and leaving behind millions of tons of rock, gravel and sand that they had sledded south.

Inexorable advance and melting retreat—this happened four times over a period of more than half a million years. But only in the fourth ice age did the glaciers move as far south as the present location of Nantucket. That was 18,000 years ago, and for nearly 10,000 years the smothering mantle of ice lay over the land. So it was as recently as 8,000 years ago—a tick of the clock in the measurement of earth's time—that Nantucket was born.

As the climate warmed again and the glacial ice thinned, cascades of melted water swept southward, carrying along the lighter detritus—the gravel and sand. This outwash, as geologists call it, formed the southern half of Nantucket, the area from Madaket along the south shore to Siasconset. And when the last of the ice melted it left behind the rest of its burden, thousands of tons of soil brought down from the north.

Look at any topographical map of Nantucket. The line of demarcation runs almost straight across the island from east to west. To the north is the terminal moraine, the small mountain range of detritus marking the southern limit of the glacier's advance. To the south is the outwash plain, the gravelly, sandy slope to the beaches along the island's shore. And if you want an even more impressive view of what Nantucketers call "the glacier's gift," ride your bicycle out the Polpis Road to Altar Rock. (A roadside marker identifies the rutted road leading to it; you can also get there by car if you go slowly over this rutted road.) There you can stand on one of Nantucket's highest bits of ground, 90 feet above sea level. Ignore the monstrous radar station blotting out much of the landscape; look east and west along the ridge of the moraine. Now turn 90 degrees. Northward the moraine extends like a plateau to Nantucket Sound. Southward the outwash plain rolls down to the beaches and the open Atlantic. Standing here, it is easy to imagine the barren hill of ecological rubbish dumped by the glacier when it melted away 8,000 years ago—just like the gravel in the snowbank when your driveway has been plowed. The giant bulldozer stopped here.

It left gravel and rubble but few boulders. By the time the glacier reached its southernmost limit, most of the biggest boulders had either been dropped along the way or ground into smaller rock in the churning motion of the moving ice mass. A few large rocks can be seen on Nantucket today, all the more evident because they are so rare compared with the rocky landscape of the New England mainland.

But what the bulldozer left, 8,000 years ago, was not an island. It was a low, rounded hill, extending many miles beyond the shores you now see on your map and from your vantage point on Altar Rock. At that time the sea was still at least 100 miles away.

The same warming climate that melted the ice now nourished the simpler forms of life. The pollen and spores of the hardiest plants, which had been carried south and had hibernated under the glacial ice, sprouted into flower. Shaggy beasts lumbered up from the southern latitudes to which their ancestors had fled before the encroaching ice. Birds came winging in to feed on the first berries, some to build their nests in the scraggly new shrubs and some to swim in the kettle holes formed by chunks of ice still melting in the hollows of the hill. And shortly afterwards came the first humans; I will tell you about them in the next chapter.

For 18,000 years vegetation took hold on the Nantucket hill. Only the toughest tundra plants grew at first, each generation nourished by the organic decay of the

previous generation. Trees began to grow among the
shrubs. You can get many conflicting arguments about
these trees. Some botanists claim that Nantucket was
once clothed by a great forest; like the geologists who
point to the strata of rock, gravel and soil to indicate the
development of Nantucket from bedrock to its present
surface, some botanists point to huge tree stumps
unearthed from Nantucket's peat bogs to support their
contention that the hill, and the later island, was once
heavy primeval forest. Others maintain that Nantucket's
winds have always inhibited the growth of its trees, especially when the sea moved in and the winds blanketed the
growing branches with salt particles. Certainly the early
settlers found wood nearly as scarce as Melville claims it
was. Perhaps there were big trees during those first 10,-
000 years of Nantucket's existence, before the killing
salt-laden winds were brought in by the sea.

It was the glaciers that also provided the sea, of course.
As they melted under the northward spread of the
warmer climate, so many trillion tons of water poured
into the ocean that the sea level of the Atlantic rose as
much as 400 feet. Were that to happen today, New
York's buildings would be inundated to the fortieth floor
(and no doubt crisis-hardened New Yorkers would only
mutter, "Oh, hell," and swim to work). Off the American
northeast coast the water crept up to what is now roughly
the shoreline of New England. Off the southeast corner
the deeper hollows between Martha's Vineyard and Nantucket were the first to fill. So as recently as 6,000 years
ago the two sandy hills became islands.

It took about another thousand years for the waters to
rise over the higher slopes off Nantucket; today these

shoals extend as far as 20 miles east and 40 miles south, and it is said that at extreme low tide you can stand with your head out of the water on some of the shoals far south of the island (you try it if you wish; I do not intend to).

As the waters moved in around Nantucket they changed the shape of the island the glacier had left behind. The outwash plain sloping for many miles to the south was assaulted by surging seas that had gathered momentum all the way across the Atlantic Ocean. Patricia Coffin described this force graphically: "A mountain of green water 40 feet high and 500 feet long, roaring in with flying mane, exerts 6,400 tons of pressure per square foot as it bombards the beach." At a rapid rate, in the measurement of geologic time, the sands of Nantucket's south shore were chewed away and spat to east and west. The island grew thinner as the south shore wore away and the eastern and western ends were built up. To the west the sweeping action of sea and sand created Smith's Point and Eel Point, with Madaket Harbor between them.

To the east the change was far more dramatic. The churning waves moved thousands of acres of sand from the south shore and laid it along the beach at the eastern end of the island. Meanwhile the storm-driven seas from the east and northeast dredged so many millions of tons of sand from the bottom of Nantucket Sound and deposited it along the island's north shore that a barrier beach stretched halfway along the length of the island. The barrier beach, now called Coatue, forms Nantucket's 8-mile-long harbor, stretching all the way from Nantucket town to Wauwinet.

That is how today's Nantucket was formed—by the ice
and the sea. And so it continues to change form, still
rapidly in geological terms. The island's south beaches
lose as much as nine acres a year. In the 19th century
more than 800 feet of shoreline was carved from the
beaches west of Surfside; much of that sand was carried
to the western and eastern points of the island. In his
History of Nantucket in 1924, Alexander Starbuck wrote:
"It is within the memory of many when the beach at
Siasconset was not over half its present width."

At Nantucket's western end stormy seas have even
formed a new island, named after the storm that created
it. In 1961 Hurricane Esther cut through a beach and
isolated a chunk of sand; dunes formed; and as of this
writing Esther Island stands in plain view off Madaket
Harbor.

I say as of this writing because another storm or the
violent action of the sea could obliterate Esther Island,
or pile up sandbanks between it and the main island until
they were joined again. This has happened to the two
other islands in the past. In the last century Nantucketers
could drive their wagons across a sand spit to Tuckernuck Island; and history records that Muskeget Island
was once joined to Tuckernuck.

In the same way the sea has drifted the sand across the
bays that once indented Nantucket's south shore. Look
at a map again and you can see how the long fingers of
water now known as Miacomet Pond, Long Pond and
Hummock Pond were once bays open to the ocean; they
have long since been blocked off by sandbars and have
become freshwater or brackish ponds.

In its gentler, slower but no less inexorable way, the

calmer waters along the island's north shore have moved the sand across bays and coves that are now landlocked ponds. We shall see how the early settlers were forced to move to the present location of Nantucket town when their first harbor was cut off from the sea; and how a sandbar, forming across the present harbor's mouth, did its part in bringing Nantucket's golden age of whaling to an end. The sand continues to shift today; the U.S. Coast and Geodetic Survey charts of Nantucket Sound were revised fifteen times during a recent ten-year period.

There is another interesting aspect of Nantucket that you will see on a topographical map: there are no rivers. This remarkable phenomenon impressed geologist Nathaniel Shaler when he studied the island in the 19th century. "This is extremely peculiar," he wrote. "There is not a single well-defined stream on Nantucket. The only approach to brooks are a few obscure channels between ponds where the water has, except in times of flood, a feeble current. The absence of streams," Shaler explained, "is due to the great porosity of the sand and gravel deposits."

So the glacier's gift, enhanced, altered and sometimes threatened by the sea, is today represented by an island about 25 miles long east to west, 6 to 20 miles wide, bounded by 55 miles of sandy shore and no more than 108 feet above sea level. And perhaps its most important characteristic is that it is an island.

You do not need a map to consider the many attractive aspects of an island, particularly an island 30 miles at sea. All you have to do is stand on a windswept beach and inhale. On the continent, particularly in the populated areas, breathing is like being the last one in the bath water. On an island it is like being aboard a ship at sea, forward of the smokestacks. When you claim that the sea air increases your appetite, you are stating a biological fact: clean air, with a higher percentage of oxygen and a lower percentage of pollutants, actually makes you healthier and hungrier.

Nearly everything is cleaned and washed on an island, more than on the mainland. But the most significant aspect of any island is the most obvious: isolation. The sense of isolation on an island contributes to the ambience if you are escaping from city life (and to the maddening boredom, of course, if you are a lighthouse keeper).Isolation has a profound influence on all life on an island—on its genetics, on its environment and on its very survival.

The first animals to come to Nantucket after the ice age walked across the valley that is now Nantucket Sound. When the waters rose and isolated them they were trapped in a new, limited environment. They could not return to the tall forests on the mainland. They could no longer migrate. Many species were, in the anthropologists' euphemism, selected out. Today there are no foxes on the island, nor are there any squirrels, chipmunks, muskrats nor—perhaps just as well—any skunks, porcupines, weasels or wildcats. Prairie dogs once inhabited—or, rather, infested—the island, but they were exterminated in 1900.

The prairie dogs had been imported, as were another example of Nantucket fauna, the white-tailed deer. The island's first deer evidently was a refugee, a buck rescued by fishermen in 1922 while he was swimming for his life several miles at sea. The buck was released on the island,

and one can imagine his reaction when after four years of lonely abstinence he discovered two does brought to the island by a sympathetic Nantucket summer resident, Breckinridge Long. Within a few years there were deer all over the island, and Nantucket's farmers were as glad as the deer hunters when an open season was proclaimed in 1935. The deer population has thus been stabilized at about 300.

Many of the island's animals have survived by evolving over the generations into species unique to Nantucket. John James Audubon, visiting the island in 1840, wrote that "there are hundreds of jumping mice, and several species of shrew and bats" seen nowhere else. On Nantucket, and nowhere else, you may find a short-tailed, tiny-eared, dumpy mouse, a small shrew unlike shrews anywhere else, a special spadefoot toad, box tortoise and snake.

And there is the Muskeget mouse. Originally a meadow mouse from the mainland, this tiny creature was isolated and forced to evolve. In succeeding generations the hardiest mutations of the meadow mouse adapted to living in the sand, burrowing into the dunes and learning to subsist on beach grass. It even discovered that when the spikes of this grass are cut, they stay green and juicy through the winter. Today's descendant of the mainland meadow mouse is a beach vole, a wholly new species.

While the rising waters imprisoned and restricted the four-legged creatures of Nantucket, it benefited the birds. As the east coast of America moved many miles inland, islands like Nantucket offered convenient stepping stones along the birds' migration routes. Virtually every species of bird following the eastern coastal flight patterns puts down on Nantucket ponds and harbors and in its trees for a respite. Brant Point is named for the thousands of brant that once flocked to this spit of land. Although the brant avoid heavily populated Brant Point now, the harbor still attracts many other varieties of ducks and geese.

But the glory of Nantucket is its flora. Not only are there innumerable species found only on the island, but there are many that exist here even when they should not. There is cactus on Nantucket, farther north than anywhere on the mainland. There is creeping snowberry, which normally grows in the much colder northern latitudes. One botanical survey indicated that the island is more a northern than a southern boundary. Of 746 species studied, more than half were usually found south of Nantucket; fewer than one-quarter were from northern latitudes. Of these species, thirty-eight were not even known north of Nantucket, and only fifteen did not appear south of the island.

Nantucket's climate, moderated by the surrounding waters and the Gulf Stream not far away, is neither too hot nor too cold. It nourishes an enormous variety of vegetation. Eugene Bicknell enumerated 1,103 different ferns; more have been identified since. Emil Guba counted 300 fungi. Some botanists claim there are more different species of plants on Nantucket than in any similar size area of America.

Nantucket's earlier residents did not help much in this process, by the way. Just as today's off-islanders desecrate the land with their Jeeps and beer cans, the first off-islanders—Nantucket's white settlers—nearly ruined the flora by turning the island into a vast pasturage for sheep. At one time there were seventeen thousand of these creatures nibbling and trampling down nearly everything that tried to grow. It took years after the sheep were finally penned up for the island to recover.

The best-known and most admired of Nantucket's flora is the heath. The heath family, including such species as bearberry, mountain cranberry and mealy plum, clothes as much as ten thousand acres of the rolling country outside the towns, and it is unique to this part of the world. Nantucketers insist on calling the countryside "the moors"—a misnomer, because a moor is more like a bog. Heath is what blankets the gentle hills and valleys, coloring it with green in spring and summer and in splashes of brilliance in autumn. There is indeed a bog on Nantucket, a cranberry bog that may be the largest in the world. This, too, is not precisely a bog by its botanical definition; more accurately it is a drained swamp.

There are Scotch heather and bayberry and wild rose and huckleberry on Nantucket's open landscape. There is Scotch broom, reportedly the gift of a visitor, Mrs. A. E. Powers, who in the 1890s sent to friends in Scotland for the seeds. She then dumped them into shoe boxes and went out across the hillsides in a pony cart, sowing the seeds by flinging them in every direction. There are subtle adaptations of mainland plant species. And—beware—there are veritable thickets of poison ivy, brilliantly beautiful in its vermilion autumn foliage but just as treacherous as in its shiny summer green.

The island environment has been kind to its flowers and shrubs but not to its trees. Whether or not there ever were huge standing forests on the island, there are none now. The reason, of course, is the wind. An island is an isolated place. It can be a temperate place; but it is usually a windy place with a special sting in its wind. The high winds of Nantucket knock down the trees that try to grow tall. The winds also carry salt spray from the ocean, encrusting the tender tips of the branches and inhibiting the trees' growth.

The island's only forest, if that is the word, can be seen in such low-lying, protected places as the area called the "Hidden Forest," near Polpis. Huddled in the hollow, the trees escape much of the wind and wind-borne salt that sweeps across the island during storms. Pines have shown some resistance to this assault by salt. But when one Nantucketer decided to save some money by importing cheaper pine seed from Europe in the 19th century, he also imported the pine tree moth, which has infested the island and hampered the pines' growth ever since. A particularly salt-resistant tree is the Japanese black pine; that, too, has recently been threatened, by the turpentine beetle. Some moderately tall elms and maples are protected by the buildings in the middle of Nantucket town. And the hardy willow tree flourishes here as it does elsewhere. A famous specimen of this tree was locally called the Napoleon Willow because two slips were brought from Napoleon's grave on St. Helena and planted on Centre Street. One Napoleon Willow blew down; its trunk was cut up and used in the landfill alongside the harbor when Easy Street was laid out between Old North and Steamboat Wharves. Salt spray coated the street. Tides washed over it. But in 1898 a willow tree sprouted in the middle of Easy Street. Traffic was routed around it until finally the tree grew so large that it threatened to block the street. It was cut down in 1935.

Out in the open, however, even the sturdiest trees are stunted by Nantucket's storms. Some of the grizzled survivors are fifty years old yet stand only 20 feet tall. Nantucket is a low-lying island; just as the seas have rounded its contours, so the winds have smoothed its vegetative topography. It is a streamlined island, on its top as well as its sides. In fact, out on what everyone calls the moors, it is almost like being at sea. Nantucket's countryside seems a continuation of the sea: the moors roll toward you in waves, the troughs and crests all in proportion as at sea. As you drive past the moors, the occasional house seems like a passing ship—high-sided and running before the wind, lifting with a wave of the land and going nearly hull-down as you pass another rise in the forever rolling landscape. Ride out on the moors and imagine yourself at sea, and you may come close to an understanding of the elemental, atavistic appeal of an island in the ocean that has attracted so many flora and fauna to Nantucket, including *homo sapiens.*

IF you will go to the Nantucket Atheneum Library, on the corner of India and Centre Streets, walk up to the main desk and look to your left, and you will see a picture that tells the whole story of Nantucket's Indians.

It is an oil portrait of the island's last male Indian. He died on November 25, 1854, two months before his

34

3
THE INDIANS

Abram Quary, from the painting in the Atheneum

eighty-fifth birthday.* In his portrait he wears his years well: his face is nearly unlined, his skin bronzed by the sun and by inheritance from his ancestors.

Look again at the face. It is the profile of a dignified old man; he might be one of Nantucket's elder statesmen. The nose is aristocratic, the chin firm. His straight white hair cascades over the morning coat he has put on for his portrait. He also wears a flowing cravat for the occasion.

But look at the floor. He has shucked off his shoes, as if unaccustomed to them, and they lie behind his chair. His trouser bottoms are tattered. His hands, too, reveal him as a man of labor. On the floor and on the table are baskets, one containing flowers, the other huckleberries. It is said that he made these baskets and asked that they be included in the portrait; the Nantucket basket is an institution, as we shall see in another chapter, and they are a legacy of Nantucket's Indians. The painting, by Mrs. Hermione Dassel, may have been done in a house on Brant Point; through the window to the left can be seen Nantucket town—a row of the white man's rooftops where once the Indians freely roamed.

His name was Abram Quary. And in his slumped posture, his dignity and the eloquent resignation in his eyes, we can read the fate of the Indians of Nantucket, after the arrival of the first off-islanders.

The story began many thousands of years before Abram Quary. The white man's ancestors came from the old world to the new by water. Abram Quary's ancestors

---

*He was in fact not the last Indian on Nantucket but the last *male* Indian. In the 19th century that was what counted. Nantucket's last female Indian was Dorcas Honorable, a servant in a white household, who died a year later.

came by land, across a ridge of tundra that linked Asia
with what is now Alaska. Over 30,000 years Abram's
ancestors filtered south and east, some to found the
Mayan and Aztec civilizations, others to inhabit the
North American continent and later to be called eskimos
(the Algonquin Indian name for "people to the north")
or Indians (because Columbus thought he had discovered India).

Archaeologists have more scientific names for the first
people in our part of the world. These early men were
already at home in the southerly latitudes when the last
glaciers started their northward retreat. And not long
after the first animals arrived on the plateau that became
Nantucket, the Indian hunters followed them.

The archaeologists call these hunters Paleo-Americans, because they belong to the Paleolithic period. Another name for them is the Fluted Point People, because
of the fluted stone points on the weapons they used for
hunting caribou and the now-extinct mastodons, saber-
toothed tigers and giant bison that had moved north to
the Nantucket area in the wake of the receding glaciers.

That was 9,000 years ago. The Paleo-Americans were
nomadic hunters, moving in small groups of one or two
families and following the migration of their prey. Evidently their sole weapon was a spear, with its distinctive
fluted point laboriously chipped from stone. They had
mastered such hunting strategies as stampeding bison
off the tops of cliffs and herding mammoths into the
quicksand of bogs; the skeletons of their prey have been
found, with their fluted-point spears still imbedded in
the remains.

Tracking their quarry northward, the Paleo-Americans

crisscrossed a hilly ridge extending from the present Long Island and Block Island to the plateaus that became Martha's Vineyard and Nantucket. Did they ever settle on Nantucket's plateau? No spears have been found on the Island. Perhaps these hunters favored the valleys when they stopped to make camp, in which case the evidence of their existence lies underwater, in the shoals off Nantucket that were once the lower-lying lands bordering the hilly terminal moraine.

The Paleo-Americans roamed the area for about 3,000 years, and not until 6,000 years ago were they succeeded by a distinctly different culture. These ancient Americans are now called the Early Archaic people. Like their predecessors they were hunters and nomads, moving with the animals they pursued. Evidently their only weapon was the spear. But the Early Archaic people were more than hunters; they were gatherers as well. Following the migrations of the animals part of the year, they settled down for short periods, gathering nuts, seeds and fruits and catching fish. They left behind a wider variety of spear points than the fluted example of the Paleo-Americans. And they made another advance in the long march of civilization: they invented a chopping tool—a knife blade made from a piece of slate. The sharpened cutting edge was round, the top edge straight to serve as a handle or, in some examples, with holes for a handle of wood or bone.

These Early Archaic people inhabited the area until about 5,000 years ago. They did settle on the Nantucket plateau. No one was sure of this until a few years ago when a Nantucketer named Lloyd Nelson, digging for quahogs in Polpis Harbor, unearthed a perfect example of an Early Archaic chopper.

For another 5,000 years, until about 100 A.D., a third group of early Americans inhabited Nantucket. They are distinguished from their predecessors as the Late Archaic people, and indeed they represented a major change; one archaeologist compares it to the Industrial Revolution. While the Early Archaic inhabitants of Nantucket still hunted with spears, the Late Archaic people invented the bow and arrow, as big an advance as the rifle that in turn succeeded it. The Late Archaic people also developed pottery—made of soapstone, for example—that was durable enough to survive until recently dug up on the island. And there is evidence that these were the first Indians to invent the pipe and to smoke tobacco. They used it for the legendary Indian pipe of peace and friendship.

They also were advanced enough to hold elaborate burial ceremonies. This is more significant than it would first appear. Some 600 centuries earlier, Neanderthal man held burial ceremonies; archaeologists know because they have identified 60,000-year-old pollen in a Neanderthal grave. Pollen means plants. Plants mean some kind of burial ceremony. And, significantly, a burial ceremony means a major difference between animal and man: the animal does not concern itself with death, does not foresee death and does not wonder about the possibility of afterlife. Man does. In a Neanderthal grave in Shanidar, Iraq, was the first evidence of this concern—a major step on the ladder of evolution from unthinking animal to thinking man.

Here on Nantucket was similar evidence that these
primitive people were concerned with afterlife. Clearly
the dead were sent off to what was considered to be
another existence of some sort. The bodies were laid out
in large areas of carefully arranged stone. Weapons and
tools were placed alongside them, to be used in the next
life. And earthen vessels were added—carefully smashed
or "killed" so they would accompany the deceased to
whatever new life fate held in store. Some of Nantucket's
Late Archaic graves also provide evidence that these ceremonies were confined to leaders of a tribe: around the
burial site were skeletons of others, presumably retainers
or servants—or wives—sacrificed to accompany the chief
to his other world.

The Late Archaic people also became island people. It
was while they inhabited Nantucket's plateau that the
seas rose and flooded the valleys to the north, cutting off
the hills from the mainland. The glaciers had retreated
nearly to the Arctic Circle, and enormous amounts of
meltwater had poured into the ocean, raising the sea
level as much as 400 feet.

But the rising waters did not cut off the Indians from
one another. For centuries they had been accustomed to
traveling overland to the areas farther north; now they
built canoes, stretching bark or animal hide over wooden
frames. At first the water they had to cross was a narrow
strip; as the sea level rose and the gap widened, the
Indians enlarged their canoes.

By roughly 100 A.D., during the time of the Roman
Empire, Nantucket's Late Archaic Indians had evolved
and advanced into what could be called a modern culture. They were very much like the Indians who were on

the island to greet the first European arrivals. They had a civilization of their own—primitive, perhaps, by present standards, but a striking advance from that of their predecessors. Some of this advancement had evolved by trial and error down the years; much of it had been brought to the island by new tribes of people from the west and the south.

This latest—and last—culture has been called the Woodland or the Ceramic-Agricultural Period. The Indians still hunted, but they farmed as well, growing corn, squash, beans and other vegetables. And they made a wide variety of ceramic implements for cooking and eating. They dug clams and oysters, which they preserved by smoking them.

They fashioned many other implements for daily life. With stone-bladed axes they cut down trees; they used fire to hollow out logs, and clamshells to scrape out dugout canoes. Paddles carved from wood propelled them around the island, up and down the harbor and across Nantucket's ponds. For the rougher waters offshore they built more modern bark or hide canoes, in which they crossed Nantucket Sound to Martha's Vineyard and the mainland.

By the time the first Europeans arrived—and gave them the name "Indians"—these American aborigines of the northeast had formed a highly sophisticated political structure. As many as thirty settlements, on the mainland and the islands, were organized into the Wampanoag Confederation. To the Great Sachem of the Wampanoag, the other tribes, each with its own sachem, pledged allegiance and sometimes paid tribute. It was a nearly feudal system in which each tribal king's rule was

absolute; at his death the authority passed to his eldest
son or, if he had no sons, his eldest daughter, who was
expected to take a royal consort.

The king or queen appointed a council of advisers,
usually elder statesmen of the tribe, and there were nu-
merous subsidiary chiefs, including pawaws, who were
prophets as well as medicine men. But absolute authority
belonged to the sachem.

His subjects were tall, dark-skinned and black-haired.
In summer they wore little besides loincloths, carrying
their belongings in shoulder bags. In winter they draped
themselves in animal skins, wrapped their feet in hides
and virtually hibernated in their wigwams.

The Wampanoag women did more than the cooking
and child rearing. They also wove beach grass into baskets, planted and harvested the crops, gathered berries,
dug shellfish and even covered the wigwam framework
after the men had constructed it. The braves were much
too busy hunting, fishing and playing games to have time
for such effeminate labor as farming. And when each
meal was ready—corn, fish, lobsters, clams, venison, oysters, always cooked over the fire on sticks or in pots—the
men ate first, then the women and children shared the
leftovers.

Brave and industrious the men were, though, especially on the water. They caught fish in large weir nets.
They built fast, seaworthy dugout canoes; some held as
many as thirty men. The first Europeans were fascinated
by the efficiency of the Indians' paddle, which propelled
and maneuvered a canoe much better than the oars of
the European rowboat.

It was the Indians' most spectacular accomplishment

on the water that would make Nantucket famous. In their dugout canoes, and armed only with bone-tipped harpoons, ropes made of tree bark and vines, and bows and arrows, they set out after the world's biggest quarry, the whale.

From the time when the water became deep enough, whales of all sizes had been seen around the island. The Indians discovered the uses of the whale—skins for warmth, blubber for food—when the huge corpses drifted onto the beaches. It became Indian tradition to divide any drift whale equally among members of the tribe. The white settlers accepted this tradition and left all drift whales to the Indians.

But the live whales sporting about the island were too much for the Indians to resist. The beginnings of Nantucket's whaling industry probably began with the 15- to 20-foot blackfish that sometimes swam into the harbor. The Indians escalated their whale-hunting until they were going out in fleets of canoes to chase the bigger whales off the south shore. Even with their churning paddles they could not outspeed a whale: but they could sneak up on one. The technique they devised remained essentially the one used for centuries thereafter, with little change even as more efficient weapons were perfected.

A particularly strong-armed and fearless Indian took up his harpoon, a long stick of wood with a sharpened blade of bone at the end. The other end was made fast to a length of rope, of twisted tree bark or particularly tough vines. The Indian harpooner thrust his weapon into the side of the whale. As the beast dashed off, or dived to the bottom, the rope was swiftly paid out. This

was the first of the legendary "Nantucket sleighrides."
For miles and hours the dugout canoe was hauled
through the water, at speeds faster than the Indians had
ever gone before, until the wounded whale began to
weaken. The other Indians in their canoes raced to keep
up; when the whale paused, they surrounded the animal
and let fly with their arrows. It often took an entire day
of pursuit and attack until finally the exhausted whale,
bristling with arrows like a porcupine, was laboriously
hauled back to the island and onto a beach. Custom
called for a gathering of the sagamores, the subchiefs,
and a rousing song. Then, under the sagamores' direction, the huge carcass was cut up and divided among
members of the tribe. Each family would hang its portion
on the side of its wigwam, to tear off pieces and boil them
for food as needed.

Try to imagine the scene: the circles of wigwams,
smoke rising from their peaks; the men sitting in groups
polishing their harpoon points, sharpening their spears
and carrying on a guttural conversation; the elders'
council in a circle, passing a ceremonial pipe; children
playing, the dogs running among them; the women bus-
tling about the wigwams, the flap doors flying up and
down as they go in and out.

Consider, too, this marvel of construction, the Nantucket wigwam, built of saplings yet sturdy enough to
stand up to an island storm. The men constructed the
framework of boughs and branches, and the women prepared the covering of animal skins. So carefully were
they interleaved, matched and tucked together that even
Nantucket's driving rain did not penetrate the shelter.

In the center of the wigwam was the cooking fire. Directly above it, at the peak of the framework, was an opening for the smoke. An ingenious lidded flap could be turned to the wind and closed against the rain or snow. Other flaps served as front and rear openings, and to provide a draft for the smoke. But not all the smoke went up through the peak, and the atmosphere inside a Nantucket wigwam, especially on a rainy day, resembled that of a smudge pot. Nevertheless, the wigwams were snug in winter and easily opened to the breeze in summer. And they were portable. If a family wanted to move to the south shore for better fishing in the summer, the animal skins could be stripped off and the light framework carried to the new location. Or it could be left in place and the skins taken to a new framework and then brought back, thereby providing an early example of the two-home family.

It was a life of labor for the Indian women, but still somewhat strenuous for the men. In addition to fishing and hunting everything from birds to whales, they played games. They had a 16th-century form of football: the ball was the size of today's handball, but the goal lines were a mile apart, and a game could go on for two or three days, with cheering sections for each team. The men also gambled, especially with dice made of painted stones. And they devoted much of their free time to another manifestation of civilization, organized warfare.

By the 17th century Nantucket was divided between two Wampanoag tribes. On the eastern end was a tribe that had come over from Cape Cod; it had a tradition of wise and powerful sachems. None of them could write; the sign of Sachem Nickanoose was   , a broken arrow. The Indians on the western end of the island had come

from Martha's Vineyard, and were led by a young sachem named Autopscot. The ill-defined border between
the two tribes was a constant source of dispute, and the
idle braves were forever preparing for and threatening
war. Skirmishes were fought over disputed farmland.
There were raids on each other's food supplies. There
was no all-out war between the two tribes, although there
nearly was on one occasion; it is the source of one of
Nantucket's first legends.

The Wampanoag were Algonquins, members of that
vast race of Indians who dominated nearly all of the
American northeast. Algonquins were great storytellers.
This was helpful because the Algonquins did not write,
and thus there was no written record of their history,
customs and traditions. The only record was the oral one
brought down through the generations. The Algonquins' storytelling tradition was not, however, so reliable
as a written record might have been. We can see this in
the legend of Wonoma:

Many moons ago there lived on Nantucket Island two
Indian tribes. The one to the east was ruled by Sachem
Wauwinet. The one to the west had as its sachem the
young brave Autopscot.

Wauwinet had a lovely young daughter named
Wonoma, known as much for her healing qualities as for
her beauty, which was exceeding fair. So great was
Wonoma's reputation as a nurse that word of it became
known on the other side of the island. One day a messen-
ger came from the western tribe with a plea from Sachem
Autopscot. A great sickness was devastating Autopscot's
people. Would Sachem Wauwinet permit his daughter
Wonoma to visit Autopscot's village and help cure the
sick?

Wauwinet met in council with his elder advisers, including the wise old Nickanoose, Wonoma's grandfather. Finally they agreed to Autopscot's request. Wonoma went among the people of Autopscot, helping and healing everywhere she went. Autopscot was grateful. He also was struck by Wonoma's beauty. And she found him handsome and wise despite his youth. Soon the sickness was over and it was time for Wonoma to return to her tribe. But before she went, she and Autopscot exchanged vows of love.

Wonoma was pleased to be back among her own people but she dared not tell her father, Wauwinet, of her love for Autopscot. There had been trouble on the border between the two tribes, and she feared that her father would be angry. Then one day there was a war council among Wauwinet's advisers. Some braves from Autopscot's tribe had been hunting in Wauwinet's territory. It was not the first time. The only answer was war. Wauwinet's braves laid plans to attack Autopscot's village the next day.

That night Wonoma slipped out of her father's wigwam, ran through the fields to the beach at Polpis Harbor and walked down the shore to Autopscot's territory, keeping along the water's edge so the incoming tide would wash away her footsteps. She reached Autopscot's tent before sunrise and warned him of the impending attack. Immediately he decided on a brave gamble. He went directly to Wauwinet. Before Wauwinet, Nickanoose and their council, Autopscot promised that he would punish the braves who had trespassed on Wauwinet's territory. He proclaimed his love for the fair Wonoma and asked for her hand in marriage. After recovering from their surprise, Wauwinet and his council

agreed. The handsome young Autopscot and the fair
young Wonoma were married and lived together happily
ever after. So did the tribes of Wauwinet and Autopscot;
and if you believe that you'll believe anything.

In short, it may or may not have happened. In Algonquin and most Indian legend (and also in our
own), the young princess is always wondrous fair and
the young sachem tall, handsome and wise for his
years. Such legends tend to overlook the facts that an
Indian princess would ordinarily be swarthy and
dumpy, and a young sachem might not be such a
prepossessing figure either. Also, princesses and sachems, like the rest of their people, regularly protected themselves against winter's cold and summer's
insects by smearing themselves with animal fat. So the
scene, if indeed it occurred, may have been somewhat
more rancid than romantic.

What we do know is that the two tribes on Nantucket
managed to avoid major conflict and bloodshed, and that
in the early 17th century there was indeed an intertribal
marriage between an Indian princess named Wonoma
and a sachem named Autopscot. We also know that,
despite occasional border flutters, Nantucket's Indians
at this time were peaceable people. When Bartholomew
Gosnold came upon the island in 1602 and went ashore
for brief exploration, he was not attacked, though he
must have been watched from behind every beach plum
bush; there were about 1,500 Indians on the island at the
time. And the first white settlers were received with unac-
countable hospitality—or, at the very least, lack of any
hostility.

The first of the white Nantucketers never did settle on

the island. He was Thomas Mayhew, and he bought Nantucket and Martha's Vineyard from William, the Earl of Sterling, who had been granted the islands by England's King Charles I, among other expressions of His Majesty's favor. Mayhew had no intention of living on a desolate outpost in the ocean; he was interested in Nantucket as pasturage for his sheep.

What is important is that he dealt honorably with Nantucket's Indians. He was careful to reimburse them for the pasturage he used, and to make sure that his flocks did not stray off the land he had rented from them. He tried to learn their language. He also attempted to act as a Christian missionary among them. At first this must have baffled the Indians, who had roughly thirty gods of their own and no doubt made invidious comparisons. But whether because of Mayhew's diplomacy or the Nantucket Indians' tolerance, they jointly agreed on and preserved a *modus vivendi*— or, more accurately, a *modus operandi* since Mayhew never lived on the island. And when he suddenly sold most of the island to a group of refugees from Massachusetts, Nantucket's Indians were hospitable even to them.

We will look more closely at Nantucket's first settlers in the next chapter. From the vantage point of the island's Indians, it was a cloud at first no bigger than a man's hand, to employ a metaphor that may come from the Indians. In the autumn of 1659 a small boat landed at the west end of the island, in what is now called Madaket Harbor. It contained a man named Thomas Macy, his wife and five children, and three young friends. They went to work constructing a shack, then settled into it for the first winter.

The Indians were interested, amused and sympathetic. Shortly the strangers' food supply ran short; the Indians gave them some of their own. Thus the new off-islanders survived their first winter. They were soon joined by their friends, the other members of the group of ten families that had purchased the island from Mayhew. Within a few years the little beachhead in Madaket Harbor had expanded into a white settlement on the bay that is now Capaum Pond. The relationship between the Indians and the white off-islanders remained friendly. What the Nantucket Indians evidently did not realize was that already they were doomed.

At first it was a slow and subtle change of affairs. The white settlers, most of them, worked at good relations with the Indians. For many years the Indians greatly outnumbered the whites. Peter Folger smoked their copper-bowled pipe of friendship and took the trouble to learn their language. Through his and Mayhew's missionary efforts, many of the Indians became Christians and formed their own congregation. The newcomers were careful to purchase land or grazing or planting rights to the land owned by the Indians, usually at the price the sachems asked. Although Mayhew had bought title from Lord Sterling, he also negotiated for and bought farming rights from the Indian sachems.

Sooner or later, though, inevitable conflicts arose. And nearly all of them could be blamed on misunderstanding more than fraud or deception. The Indians had always been accustomed to roaming freely over the island, within their tribal territories. They could not understand why they were not allowed to continue to do so. They were not building wigwams on the land they had

sold to the whites; they merely hunted on it, or let their
animals wander onto it. The white man drove them off,
and put up fences. There were no major confrontations
but there were minor ones. The white man felt cheated;
the Indian felt aggrieved.

The situation was not helped by the Indian sachems'
propensity for selling land not under their jurisdiction.
And even when they did consider it their land, they were
not always certain. Consider the case of the descendants
of the sachem Nickanoose. In a record set down by Zac-
cheus Macy in 1792, the complications are delineated as
follows.

And the said Wauwinet had two sons, the oldest was named
Isaac, but was mostly named Nicornoose, which signifies in
English to suck the fore teat; and his second son was named
Wawpordonggo, which in English is white face, for his face was

one side white and the other side brown or Indian color. And
the said Nicornoose married, and had one son named Isaac,
and one daughter; and then he turned away his proper wife,
and took another woman, and had two sons, named Wat and
Paul Noose; and when his true son Isaac grew up to be a man,
he resented his father's behavior so much that he went off and
left them for the space of near fifty years, it was not known
where. And in that time his true sister married to one Daniel
Spotsor, and he reigned sachem by his wife near about forty
years; and we made large purchases of the said Spotsors. And
then about sixty years past or more, there came an Indian man
from Nauset called Great Jethro, and he brought Judith Pad-
dack and one Hause with him, and he challenged the sachem-
right by being son to the said true son of Nicornoose.

In good faith the Nantucket settlers endeavored to
confirm the claim of great Jethro as a grandson of Nickanoose, as Nicornoose had become known to them.
Their investigation indicated that he did not appear to
be the sachem's grandson. So, Macy reported, "they held
a parley with him said Jethro, and agreed to buy all his
right, title, and property that he owned on said island, as
appears on our records." But now they discovered that
Nickanoose had also given deeds to the two sons by his
second wife, who were disdained as bastards by Great
Jethro. Confusion compounded; Indian and white settler
still more baffled and frustrated.

A modern Nantucketer who has made a study of the
island's Indians is Elizabeth A. Little. She has character-
ized the early disputes as part of a classic pattern of
conflict between planting and grazing economies. The
Indians were accustomed to growing a few crops and
letting their animals run free. The white settlers wanted
a controlled grazing economy: they were interested in
acreage and in how many animals a given area would

support. They brought in sheep, and these animals turned out to be a major source of contention between the white man and the Indian.

But Nantucket's Indians did not resort to arms, even though the white man introduced guns and gunpowder to the island. With the help of friendly whites, the Indians tried to work within the white man's system. But they were also unfortunate victims of a failing of the white man, which is to enforce moral belief by law. Just as today we persist in attempting to legalize or outlaw abortion or the use of marijuana or, in the recent past, liquor, Nantucket's settlers tried to enforce their own moral codes on the Indians. Like Sachem Nickanoose, an Indian called Nakattactonnit decided to desert his wife and take another woman into his wigwam. Disregarding Indian custom, the white settlers reacted by summoning the offending Indian to court, whose record reads: "The Sentance of the Court is that Nakattactonnit must again take his wife that he last put away and live loveingly with her or else he shall be severly whipped. Also the Sentance of the Court is that Nahkaquetan the woman that the aforesaid Indian hath kept Company withal as his wife shall be whipt Ten Stripe for Abusing of the Wif of said man."

The Indians protested in meetings with the settlers. They made formal petitions to the General Court of Massachusetts, which governed the island. White lawyers took up the Indians' case, some of them perhaps making more of it than necessary. Bureaucracy, then as now, moved slowly, far more slowly than the Indians' councils did. And the Indians continued to feel frustrated and baffled.

Their petitions to the General Court are poignant and

pitiful, no doubt partly because of the combination of
Indian illiteracy and the freewheeling grammar and
spelling of the court recorders. One complaint, in 1741,
read: "Then we the Indians of Sakdan Nantuckket for
daking away our Creddors from us and also from our
fathers but we now spake for our seuels for we know
whad haue dook away from us In time pas."

The white settlers' defense against such complaints
was equally eloquent in its own way. Responding to a
charge by an Indian named Paul Quaab, Nantucket's
selectmen answered in part: "The said Complaints are
altogether false and Groundless for we have not mo-
lested nor hindered them from planting for they Yearly
plant as much land as they want . . . and it is so far from
being true as to takeing their wood from them that we
have allow'd the Complainants and others hitherto to cut
what wood and stumps they have occasion to burn upon
Our Land that we have Purchased of their Avowed Sachems and other owners for which we have good Deeds.
. . . What occationed their Complaints Concerning Wood
was because we allowed the Indians from other parts of
the Island that had no wood to cut wood on Our Lands
above mentioned. . . . We have Great Reason to think
that s'd Paul's Petition or Complaint was first formed by
some Evil minded persons among us that makes a trade
of supplying the Indians with Rum. . . ."

Evidently, on Nantucket as elsewhere, alcohol played
an important role, or at least was useful to those who
wanted to turn the Indians' problems to their own advantage. And just as the earlier explorers had succumbed to
the Indians' syphilis, the Indians now succumbed to the
white man's rum. Answering yet another Indian com-

plaint to the General Court, the Nantucket settlers argued that the Indians "have so little Regard to their own wellfare that as Soon as their Corn is Ripe the Greater part of them for the Sake of Rum begin to make sale of it So that they are Out of Corn before the winter is past and by the Spring of Year that the English are obliged to supply them with Corn on Credit or they would go Nigh to perrish with Hunger." Here was the turn of history's wheel; it had been the Indians who had helped the first white men get through the winter.

The Indians' petitions usually were unsuccessful. Still they kept the peace, despite provocation on the island—and greater provocation from the mainland.

There the Wampanoags' famous King Philip, because of similar frustrations aggravated by armed conflict, launched King Philip's War, a bloody conflict that set back American civilization for many years. Philip himself came to Nantucket in an attempt to enlist the island's Indians in his cause.

The overt reason for his visit was pursuit of a mainland Indian who had broken a tribal law and fled to Nantucket. The situation rapidly became explosive. King Philip demanded the return of his disloyal subject. The Nantucket Indians hid him from his pursuer. And Nantucket's whites joined in protecting him.

King Philip summoned the Nantucket Sachem Autopscot and ordered him to hand the fugitive Indian over to him and to join in the war against the white man. Autopscot answered that the white settlers of Nantucket had lived up to their treaties and commitments, and Nantucket's Indians would not betray their white neighbors.

After some tense negotiations the Nantucketers of

both races ransomed the Indian refugee, and King Philip returned to the mainland. In gratitude the refugee gave up his Indian name, Assassamoogh, and assumed the name of John Gibbs. He went to school and on to Harvard, and returned to the island to settle near a pond on the eastern end of the island. There, in a settlement called Okawah, he taught young Indians to read and write. A symbol of the historic act of white-Indian cooperation can be seen today on the road to Wauwinet: Gibbs Pond, named for an Indian whose plight helped the Nantucket Indian and white man find a common cause.

But the white man's influence still contributed to the Indians' decline. More and more constricted by the settlers' growing use of the land, the Indians retreated into their tribal villages. Agreements, contracts and treaties were made, and generally honored. But each one limited the Indians' activities a bit more. The white man passed laws forbidding horses to roam the island, restraining dogs, setting areas off limits for hunting. The horses were eating the grass of the settlers' sheep, and the dogs were killing the sheep. The Indians protested that horses and dogs were part of their way of life. They also complained that the magistrates who ruled against them were too young. As Peter Folger explained, "They cannot believe that young men . . . can understand things like old men." And so it went. Hemmed in by the white men's fences, restricted by his laws—and enervated by his liquor—the Indians found their way of life sinking into slow eclipse. And the Indian population declined. The beginning of the end came with a sudden, tragic incident in August 1763.

Most of the white settlers had moved to the present site of Nantucket; a town was growing, complete with windmills on the town's highest hill. Most of Nantucket's Indians, those not working as household servants, had by now retreated to a wigwam village near Miacomet Pond. In their language Miacomet meant "at the meeting place." The center of the Indian village, with its council chamber, stood at the head of the pond. The more industrious Indians kept gardens and fruit trees and sold corn, other vegetables and fruit to the whites, many of whom paid for this produce with liquor. The entire Indian population was 358.

On August 16 a brig was sighted near the island's north shore, off Long Hill. Two sailors rowed ashore and walked across the meadow toward the town's most prominent landmarks, the windmills. Near the easternmost windmill they found the house of Joseph Quin, whose wife Molly took them in, gave them some food and asked her servant, an unnamed Indian woman, to wash their filthy clothes. The sailors explained that the brig was Irish and that it was bringing immigrants to the colonies. They returned to the brig and it sailed away. Shortly Molly Quin and her servant became sick.

The Indian woman was taken to her home in the Miacomet village. While both women lay ill, the bodies of two other women washed up on the beach near Long Hill. It became evident that they had died aboard the brig and had been buried at sea. Although no one was sure, because it was an unfamiliar disease at the time, they evidently had died of smallpox.

Molly Quin recovered. Her Indian servant did not. And by the time she died, Indians all around her were ill.

During that autumn and into the winter the illness spread through the Miacomet settlement. Some of the whites came to help nurse them, and none came down with the disease. But whatever the whites' immunity, the Indians had none. The statistics provided the grim proof: of the entire Indian population of 358, all but 100 were stricken. But of those 100 spared by the disease, only 34 were living in Miacomet's wigwams at the time; 40 Indians lived with white families, most of them as servants; and 18 were at sea, serving on Nantucket ships. Thus only 34 of the Indians who were exposed to the illness did not come down with it. But the significant statistic, the one that spelled the end of the Indian on Nantucket, was the death toll: of 258 who became ill, 222 died and only 36 recovered.

The days of Nantucket's Indians were over; it was only a matter of time before the few remnants of the once-proud tribes would die off or leave the island. Just as the Early Archaic people had replaced the Paleo-Americans, and had been replaced by the Late Archaic and Wood-land People, the Indians of Nantucket gave way to an-other culture—the white off-island settler.

The remaining Indians served out their time as labor-ers and servants. A few were excellent whalemen. By the end of the 18th century a full-blooded Indian was a curi-osity. The descendants of Wauwinet and Nickanoose were now the dregs of a new civilization.

In the spring of 1769 an Indian named Quibby was sent to jail for murder. In the jail he stabbed a fellow inmate. He was tried for both murders, convicted and sentenced to death. In the early hours of a drizzly April morning, near Newtown Gate, where Orange Street merged with Siasconset Path, Quibby was hanged. Public hangings in Nantucket were rare, so a crowd gathered for this one.

Among the people present was the wife of Quibby; her maiden name was Judith Quary. In her arms was her infant son. Judith Quary Quibby watched the hanging, betraying no emotion. But ever afterwards she insisted that her son Abram forget his father's disgraced name. Abram thereafter used his mother's name. And as Abram Quary he lived out his eighty-four years, abiding by the white man's laws with patient dignity until, as the last representative of his race, he died in 1854. The place where he kept his small, tidy cottage is still called Abram's Point, in honor of the last of Nantucket's patient, cooperative—and doomed—Indians.

Skyline of Nantucket when it was Sherburne

So we are all off-islanders, in the same sense that President Franklin D. Roosevelt once addressed the Daughters of the American Revolution as "Fellow Immigrants." Nantucket's original islanders are long gone, but they were here for nearly 9,000 years. The Nantucketers who replaced them have been here fewer than 400 years, less than one-twentieth as long.

4
THE SETTLERS

Nor was Nantucket town the first white settlement. The few families that landed at the extreme western end of the island, the area that is now Madaket, moved eastward—instead of westward like their mainland counterparts—to a small bay that served as their harbor. It is now called Capaum Pond.

Ride your bicycle or drive your car out Cliff Road, toward Madaket. You will see a tall water tower, which you should leave to your left—to port, as the Nantucketer would say. Keep going west for about three miles, until you meet what is known as the Madaket Road, joining Cliff Road from the left. Stop and look back. You have just passed an inconspicuous dirt road on your right.

Go back to this road. If you are driving, it is a good idea to park near the road and walk the rest of the way. This is one of Nantucket's deeper rutted roads; it could gouge the undercarriage of your car. And there are few areas wide enough to turn around.

About half a mile along this dirt road you will come to a rise, and ahead will be a placid body of water: Capaum Pond. Beyond it, over a rolling sand dune, you can see Nantucket Sound. Today the shores of Capaum Pond are nearly deserted, although there are a few modern houses near the beach. The rest is shrub and heath. It is difficult to believe that here was once a busy village, the first white man's settlement on Nantucket. But when you look more closely, you can see some rectangular depressions in the landscape, all around the pond. These are the cellar holes of the houses that once clustered in the settlement. They are, in a sense, the graves of the first Nantucket town.

Not one of the old houses remains at the shore of the pond. There are no ruins or artifacts for the archaeologist, only the shallow, overgrown depressions to remind us of what was there: dozens of houses and shops, with sandy paths meandering amidst them. That was when Capaum Pond was not a pond but a tidy bay open to Nantucket Sound. Gradually Nantucket's shifting sands closed the opening to the bay and turned it into a landlocked pond.

The Nantucketers of the early 17th century were far from the seafarers of later years. But the open bay was the lifeline for the fishermen and the few mariners who sailed to the mainland for supplies. When this lifeline was closed off, they were forced to move farther eastward, to the huge harbor that was already attracting some of the settlers.

They took everything with them—including their houses, down to the last piece of wood. Every house was dismantled; the beams, planks and shingles were carried to the present site of Nantucket town and the houses were reassembled there. Most were built in different configurations, instead of being rebuilt exactly as they had been at the original settlement. These first Nantucketers were not so much concerned with moving their houses as they were with reusing the wood. Wood—that was Nantucket's great scarcity, then as much as a century later when Herman Melville commented on it. And so, like Shakespeare's Birnum Wood coming to Dunsinane, Nantucket's Capaum Pond wood marched to Sherborn.

That was the name of the eastward settlement on the big harbor. Most historians today spell it *Sherburne,* but the earliest records show it as *Sherborn.* It was named after the English homeland of some of the early settlers, for intriguing reasons we shall see in the next chapter. Not until 1795 was the name Sherborn abandoned for the present Nantucket.

What brought these people across the water to make a home on a lonely island so barren that they had to transport their own wood from one settlement to another? The answer is an ancient one: religious persecution. It is an irony of the Christian religion that while it professes to teach the brotherhood of man, in fact it has down through the years taught the opposite. Christian persecution drove the Nantucketers and their parents to America. And Christian persecution drove the first settlers to Nantucket.

The first family of Nantucket—or the first family of off-islanders, depending on your point of view—was not named Coffin but Macy. We shall presently get to Tristram Coffin. But it was one Thomas Macy who was first to settle on Nantucket Island. Thomas Macy lived in Salisbury, in the Massachusetts Bay Colony. Salisbury was populated by people who had fled religious persecution in coming to Massachusetts from Europe. Now they had launched their own brand of persecution. Their chief target was Quakerism. Not only did Massachusetts Puritans abhor the Quakers, they also outlawed them. It was more than a sin to be a Quaker; it was a crime. Quakers were legally banished from the Massachusetts Bay Colony on pain of death. They were hounded from town to town, and often were mutilated and hanged.

So it was also a crime for Thomas Macy to take pity on the four Quakers who knocked on his door on a rainy April morning in 1659. In his answer to the charges against him, Macy explained that he had been out, that he had returned to find his wife ill and in bed. While he was trying to tend to her, there was a knock on his door.

He opened it to find four men, one of whom was an acquaintance and a man suspected of being a Quaker. Standing in the rain outside his door, they asked Macy for directions. The rain was severe at the moment and Macy asked them in.

He later pleaded that he told them he could not shelter them if they were Quakers; but he could not be callous enough to drive them out into the pouring rain. They stayed by his fire for a little over an hour. The rain let up; they thanked him kindly and went on their way. Word of Macy's unchristian act reached the authorities in Salisbury, and he was threatened with a fine and possible imprisonment.

Meanwhile, during the summer of 1659, friends of Thomas Macy, including one Tristram Coffin, invited him to join in the purchase of some land on an island called Nantucket, 30 miles off Massachusetts' southern coast. There were ten families in the group, and their plan was to escape the harassment of the Puritan town fathers of Salisbury by starting yet another new life on Nantucket. They were not Quakers themselves; they had no particular views pro or con Quakerism. They simply were fed up with the arbitrary and sanctimonious rule of their Puritan neighbors. And Thomas Macy had more reason than the rest of them to join the group of refugees.

Most of Nantucket Island was owned by Thomas Mayhew, who had bought the land from William, Earl of Sterling, through the Earl's American agent, James For-

rett. Mayhew lived on the nearby island of Martha's Vineyard and used Nantucket as a pasturage for his sheep.
Tristram Coffin visited Nantucket and liked its lonely
freedom. He went to Martha's Vineyard and negotiated
with Mayhew. When the haggling reached 30 pounds
sterling, Mayhew asked for an extra bonus of two beaver
hats. Beaverskin hats were the mink coats of the 17th
century in the American colonies—expensive and therefore a status symbol. Coffin agreed to include the hats.
This was a good price for a sandhill in the ocean inhabited only by Indians. The island of Manhattan had been
purchased for less than that—$24 worth of beads and
trinkets—thirty-five years earlier; possibly Nantucket's
price represented thirty-five years of inflation.

A poem entitled *The Exiles,* by John Greenleaf Whittier, depicts Thomas Macy and his family fleeing from his
house in Salisbury a few steps ahead of the authorities,
rushing to the riverbank and embarking in a "light
wherry" for Nantucket. Whittier's description has a
charming commentary on Salisbury's pastor, who dashes
to the riverbank.

> "Come back,—come back," the parson cried,
>   "The church's curse beware."
> "Curse, an' thou wilt!" said Macy,
>   "Thy blessing prithee spare."

Actually Macy's voyage was a somewhat more leisurely
process, though it was a flight from the avenging authorities nonetheless. Thomas and his wife Sarah took along
their five children and three adventurous young friends:
Edward Starbuck, Isaac Coleman (a 12-year-old orphan),
and eighteen-year-old James Coffin. Crowded into an

open boat, the exiles sailed first to Martha's Vineyard, where they put into Great Harbor (now Edgartown) for "comfort and further direction," as Macy succinctly phrased it. On they shortly went to the island just below the horizon to the south. They ran into a squall, with rain, strong winds and mounting seas, but Macy held his course for Nantucket—a wise decision considering the size of his boat; to have turned back would have meant running with the squall and spending many more hours in it. They made their landfall at the western end of the island, in what is now known as Madaket Harbor, where Mayhew had built a dock for his visits to Nantucket. And so the story of today's Nantucket, the white man's Nantucket, began.

The Macy family built a hut on the shore of the harbor. Their first tentative meetings with the Indians were friendly. As we have seen, Mayhew and his friends, particularly Peter Folger, who had learned the Indians' language, had paved the way. They had done some missionary work among the Indians, fortunately without teaching them to be intolerant of those who did not share their particular version of the faith.

Nantucket's new family had scarcely settled in by wintertime. It was a typically long, cold and dreary Nantucket winter, and Macy and his family used up the provisions they had brought with them. They would perhaps have been wiser to come to the island in spring, thereby allowing themselves time for planting, harvesting and preserving food for the winter. But had Thomas Macy stayed in Salisbury that winter, he might have wound up in jail.

Macy's Indian neighbors came to the rescue, with

dried corn, smoked meat and fish that they had stored in
baskets underground. There is little doubt that Nantucket's first white settlers would not have survived the
winter without the generosity of the Indians (with intriguing possible results: not only might Nantucket's
white settlement have been postponed for some years,
but New York City might never have had an R. H. Macy's;
through his only son, John, Thomas Macy is the progenitor of all the Macys in America).

Encouraged by the Macy example, other members of
the original purchasing group virtually rushed to Nantucket. In the next year nine more families landed in the
western harbor, built their huts and settled in. By 1663
there was a thriving community; and by 1671 there was
a settlement huddled around the bay that is now Capaum
Pond.

In the fields surrounding the settlement they planted
corn (the Indians' maize), oats and rye. The soil was not
rich enough for extensive farming. They built a gristmill
at Wesko Pond, inland from the bay; and Peter Folger,
who had been visiting the island to act as an interpreter
with the Indians, was persuaded to move to the settlement and also to serve as a miller.

Some years later, when Wesko Pond was called for
obvious reasons the Lily Pond, an eleven-year-old girl
named Love Paddock was walking home and noticed that
the pond was brimming full from a heavy rain. Love
stopped and admired the sight. She took a clamshell and
dug a little trench across the path. The water obligingly
flowed out of the pond and widened her trench so that
she had to jump across it to continue home.

While Love Paddock and the rest of Nantucket slept

that night, the dammed-up waters of the Lily Pond poured out through her trench in an ever-increasing river that soon became a raging sluiceway. The torrent swept away a fulling mill, poured into a nearby creek and rushed down to the bay and the sea, wrecking several boats along the way.

Love was awakened next morning by her father at the window crying, "Oh, what a wicked piece of work!" Wisely, she said nothing. Not until seventy years later, as death approached, did Love, then Mrs. George Swain, confess to a few friends that it was she who had caused the famous draining of the Lily Pond.

The little bay, on the other hand, blocked up, with no help from human hands. Even as a bay it was fairly shallow, but these first Nantucketers did not have large vessels; it was 1698 before the island had its first sloop. When the settlers built there, the bay opened onto Nantucket Sound, the body of water between Nantucket and the unseen island of Martha's Vineyard 10 miles north. The islanders went out mostly for fishing, and only occasionally for the hazardous trip to Martha's Vineyard or the mainland on a trading voyage.

The streets of this first settlement, if they can be called streets, were narrow sandy lanes. There were few carts, and few horses to draw them; the business of Nantucket was done on foot, by people walking the paths from house to house. The houses were square, utilitarian structures, built around a central chimney that was the essential part of the house. Architects call it a "cluster chimney," a huge, squat centerpiece to the house, with as many as half a dozen flues. The house was built around this chimney, with a fireplace in nearly every room. And the biggest fireplace of all, the altar of the early Nantucket home, was the kitchen fireplace.

You could walk into it. The fireplace took up an entire wall of the kitchen. There was, in effect, an inner and an outer fireplace. The outer fireplace included the massive hearth, with room for a chair or bench near the fire. There was an opening in the chimney that served as a baking oven. The inner fireplace contained the fire itself, with a crane suspended over it; on the crane hung the pots in which the Nantucketers cooked their meals.

The house's interior walls and ceilings were made of clamshell mortar, kept clean by layers of whitewash but usually blackened around the chimney by smoke blown back by the gusts of wind. Doors were closed to block the cold drafts. Many of the doors had "H and L" hinges, which stood for "Help, Lord," as a protection against witches.

Imagine a winter evening in one of these houses. The roar of the wind was ever-present; not only could it be heard but the drafts whistled through the walls wherever a chink had been blown out of the caulking in the outer wall. The pounding of the surf on the beach was an ever-present background noise. The driving rain came down the chimney and hissed on the hearth beneath the fire.

The family huddled near this fireplace, sitting at the kitchen table for supper—corn, beans, a bit of smoked fish—which they ate from wooden trenchers, usually with pewter spoons and two-tined forks. The only lighting came from sperm candles on the table. After dinner the family stayed by the fire, the children doing their sewing and reading at the table, mother knitting or mending in a rocking chair or sitting at the big wheel spinning wool into yarn. Father sat in the special chair in the chimney corner, smoking his pipe and looking into the embers of the fire. Early in the evening everyone dashed off to the cold bedrooms and ducked under the layers of quilts. No fires were lit in the bedrooms unless someone were ill. By morning there would be ice in the water pitcher on the bedside table, and everyone would dash again from the bedrooms to the one fire in the kitchen. Father warmed his shaving water in a sperm candle heater.

As usually happens, one of the houses in this first settlement became the central attraction. It was nearer to Hummock Pond on the south side of the island than to Capaum Pond to the north. It was the home of Nathaniel and Mary Starbuck. They converted a part of the house into a store, selling everything from "ribbining" to powder and shot, imported on Peter Coffin's sailing sloop. Most of the settlers paid cash, but some of the Indians paid for the Starbucks' goods with fish or grain, or feathers which the Starbucks sold to the settlers for their featherbeds. The Indians sometimes paid in labor, by plowing a field, mowing hay or spinning and carding wool. The Starbucks also sold cider, wine, beer and rum; but they never sold liquor to the Indians, as some of the other settlers did.

The Starbuck house was an attraction for a more important reason, and that was Mary Starbuck. She was nineteen years old, and her husband Nathaniel was twenty-seven when they were married in 1662. Nathaniel was an impressive personality, but it was Mary to whom everyone in the community turned. She was a born

leader—and a diplomat. Nearly always she prefaced an
opinion or judgment by saying, "My husband and I think
. . ." (rather, I imagine, the way Elizabeth II does today).
Mary Starbuck's house became the gathering place of the
first Nantucket settlement, the equivalent of a London or
Paris salon. Mary was called "The Great Lady," and the
Starbuck home became known as "Parliament House."
Most matters of the community were discussed here. On
some occasions the ample front parlor of the house,
which was called the great hall, was so full that windows
were opened and late-comers sat in the yard and strained
to listen to the deliberations inside. You can see this
house on Pine Street in the present town of Nantucket;
unlike most of the houses that were demolished in the
early settlement and rebuilt in today's Nantucket town,
the northern part of "Parliament House" is virtually unchanged.

While the first community flourished, a second community grew along the shores of the big harbor to the
east. The sandy trails around Capaum Pond extended
along the shoreline to the new houses and stores in the
town to the east, and soon much of Nantucket's commerce was concentrated in the village on the big harbor.
Still, the first village might have become a permanent
part of the island, had it not been for an act of nature,
part of the natural and inevitable shifting of the tides and
sand that we saw in Chapter II. The seas washing along
the north shores of Nantucket swept the sand across the
opening of the little bay, until a bar began to form across
the mouth. Then in 1700 a storm out of the northeast
drove more sand onto the bar. In that one storm the bar
rose above the surface of the water; the bay was sealed

off. Within a very few years beach grass took hold. Dunes formed. The bar became a part of the northern beach, making the bay a landlocked pond.

For a few years some of the settlers remained in their homes by the pond. But they could no longer fish, and Peter Folger's sloop could not bring in supplies for the Starbucks' store. The move was inevitable. House by house, Nantucket's first settlement was torn down and moved to the newer settlement on the big harbor.

One house remains to this day. It is difficult to find among the modern houses that have sprouted west of Nantucket town; it is south of the Madaket road and can be reached over one of the twisting, sandy paths that wind through the brush and pine trees of the area.

Let me recommend one of the best books written about Nantucket. It is a novel entitled *This Side of Land,* by a longtime Nantucket summer visitor, the late Elizabeth Hollister Frost. Often one learns more about a civilization, a culture, even a town, from a good novel than from a work of history. *This Side of Land* is a poetic evocation of Nantucket in the early 18th century, set in that last house of the early settlement. The house in the cradle, the author called it; the area of the first settlement was then called "the cradle."

It is better known as the Elihu Coleman House, but the Frost name was on the mailbox when my wife and I found our way to it in the summer of 1976. Elihu Coleman was a carpenter and a Quaker. He was also one of America's first abolitionists. He built his house in 1722. In 1729, sitting by the huge fireplace that is still there, he wrote a treatise entitled *A Testimony Against That Anti Christian Practice of Making Slaves of Men.* Not a great deal

of attention was paid to Elihu Coleman and his treatise
at the time. But a century later, when abolitionism was
an article of faith among many New Englanders, one of
the foremost abolitionists, William Lloyd Garrison,
made a pilgrimage to the Elihu Coleman house to honor
one who had lit the torch so long before.

At that time the house was still owned by a Coleman,
Elihu's son. But as the years passed it was deserted. The
windows were boarded up. Animals and birds took refuge in it. Elizabeth Hollister Frost bought it just in time
to preserve and restore it; today it stands on its hill facing
south across miles of open heath and huckleberry, a symbol of the cradle of Nantucket.

Oddly, Nantucket's cradle did not produce its first
baby until 1663, four years after the arrival of the first
settlers. By that time more than a dozen families had
settled on the island. The first Nantucket-born white
child was the daughter of Nathaniel and Mary Starbuck,
and she was named after her mother, the Great Lady.
Once Nantucket's population began to increase, a population explosion took place. Each birth was an important
affair, attended by most of the women in the community.
One announcement of the arrival of a new Nantucketer
was accompanied by the news that "Mother, Sister
Susan, Aunt Mary, Cousin Hepsibeth and eleven other
women came in, and most of them spent the night."

The grand progenitor of Nantucket was the leader of
the original ten purchasers of the island, Tristram
Coffin. He became the acknowledged head of the community; we shall see more of him and his administration
of the island's affairs in the next chapter. But even if
Tristram Coffin had played no part in the development
of the early Nantucket community, he left his mark on

the island many times over, by his contribution to its population.

Tristram and Dionis, his dutiful and prolific wife, had nine children and seventy-four grandchildren. By 1728, less than a century after Tristram's arrival on the island, the number of his descendants had reached 1,582, of whom 1,128 were still living. A century later one Sir Isaac Coffin, a descendant of Tristram, came to Nantucket Island from his home in England. A rare Coffin, he was childless (or at least presumed to be childless; he was a bachelor). His mission to Nantucket, he said, was to do something for the Coffin clan. He decided to found a Nantucket school for Coffin descendants; it developed that fully half of the island's population could prove they had Coffin blood.

Some of the other original families were nearly as prolific. During the first hundred years there were not many new arrivals from the mainland. The first families' children and grandchildren intermarried. In similar situations, with a few families multiplying in an isolated location, the result often has been a high degree of retardation, albinism and other effects of inbreeding. Nantucket has had its share of retardation. The Newbegin sisters who lived in squalor in their shack were perhaps the most famous examples. There have also been a good many cases of deaf mutism and insanity (one was known to everyone as "Mad Tucker"). And it was claimed at one time that it was difficult to select an unprejudiced jury on Nantucket because so many people were interrelated; as a result, all appeals from the Nantucket court were heard in Boston.

But if there was one clear result of Nantucket's combination of isolation and inbreeding, it was eccentricity.

Even by New England's standards of odd behavior, Nantucket fostered some notable examples of eccentricity (which Nantucketers called "a queer craft"). In fact, it has been claimed that normal behavior on Nantucket was not precisely the same as elsewhere. One off-islander recalled in recent times a word of warning from a future father-in-law: "My daughter, sir, has in her veins some of the blood of all the original settlers of Nantucket, and a queerer lot God never made. So be prepared for anything."

Perhaps it was just as well that the sands blocked the mouth of Capaum Pond, because it would not have been deep enough for the vessels that the Nantucketers were using by the end of the 17th century. By that time Nantucket had already begun the business on the great waters that would make the island famous.

Like the Indians, the Nantucketers had been watching the whales that sported and spouted off the island. The Indians had perfected their whale-catching technique, described in the previous chapter, before the white settlers arrived. And when in 1672 a small whale, called a "scragg," blundered into Nantucket's harbor, the Indians showed their new neighbors how to catch it and cut it up.

Whaling did not originate on Nantucket Island. Both Indians and whites had been going out in boats after the big quarry all along the New England coast. So the same year, 1672, that the Nantucketers caught their first whale in the harbor, they made overtures to a man named James Loper, a veteran whaleman on Cape Cod, to come to the island and teach them his skills. Evidently nothing came of this offer; there is no record of Loper coming to the island. But the Nantucketers persisted. There is a

legend that one day when a number of whales were rolling and diving off the south side of the island, a Nantucketer pointed to the open Atlantic and said, "There is a
green pasture where our children's grandchildren will go
for bread." Another Cape Codder, Ichabod Paddock,
was approached; he came to Nantucket. With his help the
islanders began to harvest the green pastures off their
shores.

Whaleboats were built. Harpoons and lances were
fashioned. Some of the Indians were recruited. Soon
there were clouds of black smoke swirling over the town
as trypots blazed on the beach. The smell of burning fat
spread through the community. Barrels of whale oil were
rolled into warehouses, to be shipped to Boston and
eventually to London. Nantucket's great industry was
born.

At first the whaleboats were launched from the
beaches along the south shore. The whalemen went farther and farther to sea to chase the lumbering beasts;
some used larger sloops instead of whaleboats. Inevitably one of them, Christopher Hussey, was overtaken by
a storm and blown far to the south, beyond the shoal
waters around the island. Hussey and his crew managed
to ride out the storm, then turned for home. But before
they left the deep water they came upon a bigger, square-
built whale, unlike any they had seen near the island.

It was a sperm whale. Hussey and his men got a harpoon into it, killed it and hauled it back to the island. The
rich, pure spermaceti of this whale made Hussey and the
other Nantucket whalemen realize that there was a far
richer harvest out in the deep ocean than anything they
had found before. The year was 1712, the opening of a
new era for Nantucket.

Jethro Coffin House

THE new town to which the early Nantucket settlers moved was called Wesko, then Sherborn, and finally Nantucket. It was on a rise of the island's terminal moraine; windmills were built on the high part of this rise, and so was a house that we shall now go to see.

It stands on Sunset Hill, named no doubt for the magnificent sunsets that can be seen across the moors toward

5
THE GREAT FEUD

famous 'wishbone chimney' from the 'oldest house' (1686)

Madaket, Tuckernuck and the open water. The house is striking, partly because it has been restored in a parklike setting. It is handsome, at least to those who admire the harmonious lines of early functional architecture. It is at once a symbol, an evocation and possibly a fake.

Although proclaimed Nantucket's oldest house, it may not be. Praised as a pristine example of the architecture of the 17th century, it may not be that either. It is called the Jethro Coffin House; that it is, a symbol of one of Nantucket's most intriguing periods, in which a family feud virtually turned the island into armed camps.

We will come to that. But first, the house.

The exact date of its construction is not known. But it

was almost surely built no earlier than 1686. Accordingly, it is a subject of some controversy, because it might not be the oldest house on Nantucket. There are a couple of other contenders in Siasconset; we will take a closer look at them in Chapter XI. They may have been built as early as 1675 and 1681. You can get into a good argument over these conflicting claims, and perhaps the dispute will never be resolved. Suffice it to say that the houses at Siasconset were originally fishermen's shacks, so the Jethro Coffin House certainly qualifies as Nantucket's oldest year-round home.

But there is also a question about whether or not it is the house it once was. It has been painstakingly restored, even including a well sweep that may or may not have been part of the original. The interior of the house, like all those of the 17th century, is built around an enormous cluster chimney. The central room is the kitchen, with its huge fireplace where family life centered. The other main rooms are grouped around the central chimney, with a fireplace for each room. The interior may be closer to the original than is the exterior.

Have you ever noticed the difference between most American reconstructions and reality? In many period movies, for example, everyone's clothes are a little too clean, things seem new and there are few distractions. The director has presented not reality, or even as close an approximation as he can produce, but a slightly idealized version—not so much what it was like as what he would like it to be like, or what he thinks you would like it to be like. The Coffin House may be a good example of this.

Let me recommend another book: *The Architecture of*

Historic Nantucket by Clay Lancaster. He reports a most interesting exchange between some of the principals during the restoration of Nantucket's "Oldest House" in the 1920s, and in the process has stimulated an interesting controversy.

By the 1920s the ancient house on Sunset Hill had fallen into considerable disrepair. The Nantucket Historical Association finally came to its rescue and bought the house in 1923. The association engaged the services of an expert on such old structures, William Sumner Appleton, Corresponding Secretary for the Society of New England Antiquities. Mr. Appleton conducted an exhaustive study of the house and came to a conclusion that surprised and somewhat dismayed the Nantucketers.

Among the aesthetic attractions of the "Oldest House" are its clean lines, with the austere, flat facade and the roof rising to a peak and swooping down in a long pitch to one-story height in the rear. On the mainland this design is generally called a saltbox house; it is rarely called that on Nantucket, where the more picturesque British term "catslide roof" is preferred. Nantucketers also call it a lean-to house, since the crude early fishermen's shacks were built this way.

But what Appleton concluded was that the original Coffin House evidently did not have these clean, straight roof lines at all. It may have had the long slope in the back—although that, too, could have come later—but the front part of the roof was apparently broken by two triangular gables with windows in them. On December 28, 1925, Appleton wrote to William F. Macy, President of the Nantucket Historical Association: "I strongly incline to the opinion that investigation will show that

there were in this house what might be called front
dormer windows, and that these constituted the main
sources of light for the two chambers."

Dormer windows marring the simple, dignified facade
of this beautiful old house? Mr. Macy passed along this
disturbing discovery to one Winthrop Coffin, who, it
happened, was financing the restoration. Mr. Coffin replied with some diplomatic displeasure. "I suppose an
investigation of the roof timbering would show conclu-
sively whether or not such windows were there originally. Personally, I rather like the looks of the plain
roof," he wrote, adding politely, "I'm sure that Mr. Appleton would not advise putting the windows in unless
the evidence of their earlier existence was 'absolute.' "

Mr. Macy could take a hint, particularly from the man
who was paying the bills. "I recognize Mr. Appleton as
an authority," he wrote Mr. Coffin. "But unless he is
insistent on this point, I personally should be inclined to
leave the roof as it is, and I hope that he will waive that
point."

Evidently Mr. Appleton could not provide "absolute"
evidence. The architect for the restoration, Alfred E.
Shurrocks, worked with Appleton; and Shurrocks' plans,
dated August 1927, included the dormer windows in the
front roof. But when the restoration was completed in
1929 there were no dormer windows marring the facade
of the "Oldest House."

Nor was there a porch. As the author of *The Architecture
of Historic Nantucket* points out, gabled dormers like the
ones indicated for the Coffin House would have funneled
water down the front of the building so that a porch and
a roof would have been required over the doorway; oth-

erwise everyone going in and out of the house would have been drenched in a veritable cascade on any of Nantucket's frequent rainy days. Whether or not the architects found indisputable proof of the dormer windows, there was the word of a Coffin who had lived in the house that in the 19th century it had "an extensive wooden porch."

Against this evidence is the valid contention that the rafters of the roof had been replaced so often no one could tell for certain what the original construction had been. In short: an intriguing argument without proof. In any case, the house you see on Sunset Hill today is a strikingly attractive example of early Nantucket architecture, lovingly restored to what may or may not have been its original form. The most impressive feature of the house is the massive central chimney. That alone is a masterpiece of reconstruction, even including a design at the top that has mystified everyone who sees it.

To some it resembles an upside-down horeshoe; another name for the building is the "Horseshoe House." Others think it is a wishbone. More likely, it is a provincial copy of the Jacobean chimney design popular at the time.

There are some who like to think that the curious design was meant to evoke the union of two families. It is a pardonable assumption. For this house does indeed symbolize the end of what was Nantucket's bitterest interfamily feud.

The house was built for Jethro Coffin, grandson of the original Tristram, and Mary Gardner, whose father John Gardner was Tristram Coffin's implacable enemy. Indeed, if the Montagues and the Capulets had joined to build a villa for Romeo and Juliet, it would not have been more surprising than the marriage of Jethro Coffin and Mary Gardner, and the wedding present of the Jethro Coffin House.

The Coffin-Gardner feud was not one of ancient bloodlines, as in Verona. It was not a religious confrontation, as in Salisbury. The Coffins and the Gardners differed, to understate the case, on political rather than family or religious grounds. Yet the Coffin-Gardner conflict precipitated antagonism, vindictiveness and persecution as great as that of any religious or blood feud, and it went to the heart of the political structure of Nantucket.

Tristram Coffin was something of an aristocrat, and even more an autocrat. *Patronymica Britannica* traces the Coffin name in England back to a man named Colvin or Colvinus, who was granted land by Edward the Confessor. Tristram's grandfather sided with William the Conquerer, and was presented with Brixton Manor, in Devonshire, for his services on the battlefield. Tristram was in his twenties when Cromwell's Roundheads seized Brixton Manor, causing him to flee to the colonies.

In America Tristram Coffin supported a large family of refugees, including a widowed mother and two aunts. At first he and his wife Dionis ran a tavern in the town of Newbury, a stop-off point on the road from Boston to the northeast area that later became the state of Maine. But as he watched the New England Puritans more and more resemble Cromwell's men, Tristram Coffin decided to strike out again and found his own dynasty in the New World.

From the start he was acknowledged as the leader of

the original Nantucket settlers. In his view they were not only leaving Salisbury because of its unpleasant atmosphere but were forming their own political structure in their new home.

They had bought the island, Tristram Coffin reasoned, so they could live under whatever conditions they preferred. And Tristram Coffin tended to assume that what he preferred was what everyone else preferred—or damned well should prefer. The original ten families had scarcely settled on the island when they elected him their equivalent of governor or mayor. To Tristram Coffin, it seemed only his due.

For the first few years all went well, in Tristram Coffin's view. The little settlement grew. His authority became unquestionable. Mary Starbuck, the Great Lady, was the one to whom many turned for advice, and her influence was considerable. But Tristram Coffin was the one who made the important decisions.

It was perfectly legal, if not democratic as we would define the term today. For one thing, Tristram Coffin and his family dominated the town's elections. Under the original settlers' agreement only the first purchasers could vote; each had two votes. Two of Tristram's sons and one son-in-law had chosen to stay on the mainland; one son, Peter, owned timberlands in New Hampshire and made a tidy profit shipping lumber to build houses on Nantucket. Tristram Coffin cast two absentee ballots for each of these mainland family members whenever there was a Nantucket election or referendum.

But it became apparent that some new blood was needed on the island. New muscle, to be more precise; tradesmen and craftsmen were required to do some of the town's work. So the settlers made a decision that was to haunt them for nearly a century: they voted to attract some off-islanders for certain types of work and service. The inducement was a "half-share," whereby each newcomer would be granted one vote—as against an original purchaser's two—and half as much land as each original settler was entitled to. In 1672 one William Bunker agreed to come to the island and construct a mill. Samuel Streeter came to be a tailor, Nathaniel Wyer a farmer, Joseph Coleman a seaman, John Savage a cooper, John Bishop a carpenter, Joseph Gardner a shoemaker. And on August 5, 1672, Joseph Gardner's brother John signed a contract agreeing to leave Salem and come to the island to "set up the trade of fishing." Within two years John Gardner would lead a revolt of these "Half-Share Men," as they became known, to wrest authority over the island from Tristram Coffin and his fellow Proprietors, as they called themselves.

It is difficult to find a book on American history in which the author does not quote a Frenchman named Hector St. John de Crèvecouer, who lived in the colonies and wrote graphically about the lives and times of Americans at the turn of the 18th century in his famous book *Letters of an American Farmer.* In fact, Crèvecouer wrote a great deal of nonsense about America, and one of his least perceptive reports came during a visit to Nantucket. He did provide, with a reporter's eye, many details of the daily lives of the islanders, and offered an authentic description of the island itself. His prose had its own flavor: "My nostrils involuntarily inhaled the saline vapours which arose from the dispersed particles of the foaming billows or from the weeds scattered on the shores." This

is one of the more involved attempts to describe Nantucket's air. But his major observation concerning the
island was considerably flawed.

Crèvecouer wrote that since the time of the first settlement on Nantucket Island "all has been a scene of unin-
terrupted harmony. Neither political nor religious broils;
neither disputes with the natives nor any other conten-
tions, have in the least agitated or disturbed its detached
society."

Reality was rather different. In fact, Nantucket at this
time was a hotbed of dissension. For their part, the Half-
Share Men had concluded that they were virtually the
victims of a conspiracy: they had agreed to come to the
island to supply much needed services but they found
they were second-class citizens. They had one vote while
the first settlers had two. They could have only half as
much land. They were discriminated against in other
ways. And clearly they were indispensable to the community. But what rankled more than all their other griev-
ances was the arbitrary rule of Tristram Coffin and the
other self-appointed proprietors of the island. Nantucket, in the view of the Half-Share Men, was in effect
a fiefdom of Tristram Coffin, his family and his friends,
accomplished through rigged votes. Give each man one
vote, the Half-Share Men concluded, and you would
have an equitable society in which the majority, not the
oligarchical minority, would decide what was best for
Nantucket and its people. What was needed to accom-
plish this change was a leader. The arrival of John Gardner provided that leadership.

The situation had a different complexion to most of
the original settlers, and particularly to Tristram Coffin.

In their view the Half-Share Men had signed a contract agreeing to subservient status. Now, unaccountably and inexcusably, they had decided to break that contract. The original purchasers had established the community. They had endured hardship and had not only survived but had made Nantucket what it was. In the process they had hired these off-islanders to assist them. Now the helpers wanted equality with their employers, and their betters. Moreover, they reasoned, such subversive thoughts probably never would have occurred to them had it not been for this newcomer, John Gardner. He had been on the island only two years when the revolt started; unquestionably he was a rabble-rouser and a troublemaker.

John Gardner and Tristram Coffin became spokesmen for opposite points of view and implacable antagonists. The islanders divided between Coffin and Gardner factions. Soon the Gardner faction found itself presented with an opportunity—not on Nantucket Island but across the ocean in London.

Charles II handed over to his brother James, the Duke of York, a huge section of the American colonies, including Long Island, the Elizabeths, Martha's Vineyard and Nantucket. The Duke of York promptly appointed his friend Sir Francis Lovelace governor of the area, and sent him to New York.

Governor Lovelace methodically requested all holders of patents and purchasers of land to record or confirm their holdings within his jurisdiction. At that point a minor mischance threatened the authority of Tristram Coffin and the original ten purchasers.

As we have seen, Thomas Mayhew had purchased

Nantucket from the Earl of Sterling, and had in turn sold it to Tristram Coffin and his nine partners. The Nantucket purchasers were now requested by the new governor to confirm their ownership of the island by submitting proof of purchase, in the form of a deed. They turned to Thomas Mayhew. To their dismay, he admitted he had never received his deed.

Mayhew had made his purchase through Lord Sterling's agent, James Forrett. But it happened that Forrett had been recalled to London shortly after the deal had been concluded and had neglected to send the deed to Mayhew. Knowing that he had concluded a bona fide purchase, Mayhew had not been concerned. Nor was he now; he simply asked New York for a copy.

Meanwhile, in the spring of 1671, Tristram Coffin and Thomas Macy sailed to New York to meet the new governor and present their credentials. Governor Lovelace accepted them and agreed to their claim to the island—provided, of course, that it was backed by proof that Thomas Mayhew, who had sold the island to them, could prove his ownership at the time.

The problem was that the clerks in Governor Lovelace's office could not find the deed.

Thomas Mayhew was now eighty-three years old, a vigorous and impressive man. He went immediately to see Governor Lovelace. The governor was persuaded that Mayhew spoke the truth, but without any record of the deed, what could he do?

Mayhew was thunderstruck. After thirty years of assuming—and knowing—that he had acted in good faith, he could not return to the islands and tell Tristram Coffin and the other purchasers that they might not legally own Nantucket. Instead, Mayhew made a desperate appeal to a man he knew, a veteran clerk in the governor's office. The man's name was Mathias Nicholls. If anyone knew his way through the mare's nest of the governor's archives, Nicholls did.

Nicholls reluctantly agreed to undertake a tedious search through the provincial archives. It took months, but at last he found the deed, properly signed and sealed by Lord Sterling's agent James Forrett.

Mayhew took the deed to Governor Lovelace, who promptly issued the proper patents confirming the claim of Tristram Coffin's ten purchasers. It was agreed that the annual tribute would be four barrels of codfish.

John Gardner and his followers thereby narrowly

missed out on their first chance to upset Tristram Coffin
and the other proprietors. But they lost no time taking
advantage of the agreement with the new governor. In
the spring of 1673 they volunteered to deliver the annual
tribute of four barrels of codfish. While in New York they
arranged an interview with the governor and ingratiated
themselves with him. On their return they had some
disturbing news for Tristram Coffin: Governor Lovelace
had decreed that hereafter on Nantucket every man
should have an equal vote.

And there was a further slap in the Coffin face. The
governor had agreed to a new name for the growing
settlement on the big harbor. John Gardner had suggested Sherborn, and Governor Lovelace readily consented. What was galling to Tristram Coffin was that
Sherborn was the name of the Gardner family homestead
in England.

Tristram Coffin was not the sort to take something like
this without a fight. He turned to his old friend Mayhew,
from whom he and his friends had bought the island, to
intercede with the governor. Mayhew felt that he was not
up to another expedition to New York, but he dispatched
his son Matthew. In Long Island Sound, en route to New
York, Matthew met with a ship whose skipper had aston-
ishing news: the Dutch had attacked New York and had
retaken it from the British; Governor Lovelace had fled
to London.

Tristram was not beaten yet. He sent word to all the
immediate family members of the original purchasers,
wherever they were. Everyone must gather on Nantucket
in a show of force, to keep the island from being taken
over by the Half-Share Men. One who heard Coffin's call

was as far away as Barbados. He was Stephen Hussey, son of original purchaser Christopher Hussey. Stephen had made a fortune in Barbados, and now he wanted to see his family's land on Nantucket. Stephen was also a lawyer, and when he saw the opportunities for litigation on Nantucket, he decided not to return to Barbados. In the years to come Stephen Hussey would be the Indians' best friend in court, perhaps a bit more of a litigious friend than the Indians needed.

Tristram Coffin was still mustering his supporters when the tide turned again in New York. The English recaptured the city and a new governor, Sir Edmund Andros, took office. Tristram Coffin appealed to him, stating the case for status quo on Nantucket: one man one vote—except, of course, for the Proprietors, who should have two. Andros agreed with Coffin.

Meanwhile events on Nantucket moved ahead on their own. So bitter had the two factions become that a simple misunderstanding, one that might normally have called only for a judicial ruling in New York, erupted into recrimination, defiance and repression.

Thomas Macy was Nantucket's Chief Magistrate, under a one-year commission from the governor. On October 1, 1676, Macy's commission expired. Preoccupied with other matters, Governor Andros did not immediately renew the commission or appoint another chief magistrate. Accordingly, Macy called a town meeting, in which it was voted that he would continue to serve until his successor was named by New York.

Thomas Macy was one of the Coffin faction. But the Clerk of the Court was Peter Folger, who had joined forces with John Gardner. This same Peter Folger, who had done missionary work with the Indians and who had been invited to Nantucket to set up a mill, was one of the island's most respected leaders, and probably its most learned man. Folger now decided that Thomas Macy was serving illegally; therefore he would not turn over his court records, nor would he serve any longer as clerk.

The town met again, in raucous confrontation. The vote—corn kernels for yes, beans for nay—supported Macy. Folger was requested again to hand over the court records. He refused. He was sentenced to jail.

The jail—or "the gaol," as some Nantucketers like to spell it—that is one of the exhibits of the Nantucket Historical Association is a more recent correctional facility, if it may be called that. It was built in 1805, of logs bolted with iron; its sides were sheathed with pine and shingled. The windows are heavily barred. Two of the cells have fireplaces. Peter Folger's jail was less pretentious, nor could it be regarded as maximum security; one prisoner is said to have complained that if the town did not do something to keep the sheep from wandering in, he would leave. Evidently prison breaks were not a major concern at Nantucket. When asked if she were nervous because of her association with hardened criminals, a Nantucket jailer's wife responded, "Certainly not. I'd have you understand they are all our own people, and perfectly respectable."

Peter Folger did not consider his fellow inmates particularly respectable, evidently, nor did he think much of Nantucket's jail. He complained to the governor. Andros was still preoccupied. John Gardner decided to make an issue of Folger's cause. Gardner was summoned to court. He refused to appear and was forcibly brought in. He

treated Magistrate Macy with contempt, even refusing to
take off his hat. Gardner was disenfranchised and fined.
Howls of indignation arose from the Garnder faction.
Increasingly repressive measures were instituted against
the Half-Share Men by the Coffin faction. When Gardner
refused to pay his fine, the Coffin people seized half a
dozen of his cattle. Finally Governor Andros was forced
to take action.

This time, perhaps feeling that Tristram Coffin and his
people had gone too far, the Governor took Gardner's
side. He canceled Gardner's disenfranchisement and
took the Folger case under advisement. Evidently taking
a cue from New York, the next town meeting reinstated
Gardner's rights and elected him to the town council.
Folger was freed. And in a handsome gesture of compromise, they elected Tristram Coffin Chief Magistrate.

The great feud appeared to be waning, if only because
both sides must be tiring of the endless wrangling. A
degree of harmony seemed to prevail. And then Tristram Coffin made his big mistake.

He was seventy-three now, an old, cantankerous and
feeble man. In 1678 a French brig was shipwrecked on
Nantucket's shoals. As Chief Magistrate, Tristram Coffin
was supposed to oversee the salvage of the wreck and its
contents. But he delegated the chore to some friends,
and evidently they were friends in need; most of the
contents of the shipwreck disappeared.

The situation was reported to New York and in due
time Governor Andros sent a Board of Admiralty to investigate. They found that Tristram Coffin had acted
"contrary to law," and declared that he must make resti-
tution in the amount of £342.

This in the 17th century was an enormous sum. Tristram Coffin had been autocratic, even repressive. But he had never profited from his authority. And there was no indication that he had shared in the illicit gain his friends had made from this shipwreck. Now, a broken man, he came before the town court to plead for a reduction in his fine. He did not have the money. A fine of this size, he said, would bankrupt him.

It happened that during these proceedings, which had dragged on for two years, Tristram Coffin's term as Chief Magistrate had expired; his successor was none other than John Gardner. And in the deliberations over the fine, the person who argued most convincingly to spare the beaten old man was John Gardner. The fine was reduced to £150.

Tristram Coffin died a year later. The other members of his faction gave up the fight. In their view the upstarts had at last won. Nantucket's elections now had one vote for each man (women's suffrage would not come until 1920).

There would be echoes of the feud in later years. In 1795 a robbery at the grandly named President and Directors and Company of the Nantucket Bank caused the whole town to become embroiled in controversy, and similar factions formed to accuse each other; finally it was discovered that some off-island visitors were the culprits. A decade later the Proprietors battled the Half-Share Men in what became known as the "Sheep War," a bitter dispute over grazing rights. But the Coffin-Gardner family feud was over.

John Gardner died in 1706. He lived to see the wedding of his daughter Mary to Jethro Coffin, Tristram's grandson, in 1686. Mary was sixteen years old and Jethro was twenty-six. The house was a wedding present from the two families: Jethro's father Peter supplied the lumber from his New Hampshire mill, and John Gardner provided the land. In fact, there was a last-minute hitch when Peter Coffin discovered that there was no deed to the land, and refused to supply the lumber until it was produced; John Gardner rushed to the town record-keeper and found the deed.

If you climb the stairs of the Jethro Coffin House, you will see at the top of the narrow staircase the headstone from John Gardner's grave, brought here from the island's Burying Grounds. In the upper chamber is a portrait of Mary Gardner, presumably a good likeness. Mary made four trips to Boston (the equivalent of a trip to India today) to have it painted. She died at ninety-seven, outliving her husband by forty-one years. Look at the stern eyes and the Gardner jaw in Mary's portrait, and perhaps you can understand why even Tristram Coffin met his match when John Gardner came to Nantucket.

the Rotch Counting House, fountain in front

COME down Sunset Hill. Walk along Main Street to the cobblestoned square. At the foot of the square is a red brick building with a sign over its door: "SHIPS DARTMOUTH, BEAVER, ELEANOR." This building is still known as the Rotch Warehouse, or the Rotch Countinghouse, al-

6
CROSSFIRE OF
THE REVOLUTION

William Rotch, 1734-1828

Francis Rotch's ships in Boston Harbor, the Boston Tea Party, Nov. 28, 1773

though it is no longer a warehouse or a countinghouse and is no longer owned by a Rotch. The building was the center of Nantucket's early whaling days, when the town's central figure was a man named William Rotch.

Nantucket's square is so-called because it is the business center of the island, not because of its shape, which is rectangular. At one end of this rectangle stands William Rotch's countinghouse; at the other end is the Pacific Bank. The two buildings reflect two distinct periods in Nantucket's whaling history: the early, hard years interrupted by two wars, and the later years of "greasy luck" and glory. Each looks its part—the spare, utilitarian Rotch building of the struggling beginnings and the porticoed, opulent bank of the golden age. One represented the Atlantic Ocean, where Nantucket's whaling started; the other carries the name of the Pacific, whence came Nantucket's greatest prosperity.

We will look at the latter period in the next chapter. Let us start properly at the beginning, at this spare and handsome structure strategically situated at the foot of Main Street and at the head of the wharves.

The building is not exactly what it was. The pitched roof was once a gambrel roof, for a practical New England reason: taxes were assessed on the number of stories in a building, and by having a gambrel roof on his warehouse William Rotch managed to get more storage space in the attic, which as a partial story was not taxed. The building was gutted in the fire of 1846, and in the course of its restoration the present roof was substituted.

A canny businessman, William Rotch (pronounced *Roach*) was also a great deal more. He was Nantucket's first great whaling merchant and whaleship owner; he was the island's spokesman in many difficult wartime negotiations between friend and foe; and as a pragmatic Quaker and pacifist, he became the conscience of Nantucket.

He was a second generation Nantucketer. His father, Joseph Rotch, came to the island in 1734, with no funds but with plenty of ambition. Joseph Rotch set himself up as a shoemaker and later married Love Macy, great-granddaughter of the original Thomas Macy and daughter of a Coffin.

Joseph Rotch promptly made the most of his good connections. He became a shipping merchant, sending vessels with whalebone, codfish and other Nantucket produce to the West Indies, to bring back rum and brandy, sugar and molasses. But as his fortunes expanded he looked back to the mainland, investing in acreage along the Acushnet River near a town that was then called Dartmouth and is now called Fairhaven.

There was a sad irony to Joseph Rotch's financial prosperity on Nantucket. He and his wife Love had thirteen children; only three survived childhood. Then, in 1767, his wife died. Joseph left the island and went to Dartmouth where he started a shipyard, and included housing for his workers. He named the new Rotch settlement Bedford; and thereby a Nantucketer founded a town that eventually, under the name of New Bedford, superseded Nantucket as a whaling port.

Joseph Rotch's three surviving children were sons: Joseph Jr., Francis and William. As they became old enough to go to work, young Joseph stayed in Bedford with his father; Francis went to Boston, where he could look after Rotch shipping interests; William returned to his birthplace.

William's timing was excellent. He arrived on the is-

land at a point when whaling had become the business
if not yet the industry of Nantucket. The boats that had
gone off the island to chase whales spotted from the
shore had given way to whaleships that went down the
Atlantic to search out the oil-rich sperm whales of the
southern waters. No longer were the carcasses towed to
Nantucket's beaches. Now narrow platforms were built
on the ships' sides and the whales were cut up at sea,
then rendered into oil in trypots on deck. The oil was
brought back to Nantucket in barrels, to be shipped out
to London, which was Nantucket's biggest customer.

Nantucket whaling was in its infancy but already was
hugely profitable, and William Rotch plunged into it.
Soon he was dispatching ships, some of them constructed in his father's yards along the Acushnet River,
to pursue the sperm whale throughout the Atlantic.
Other Rotch ships sailed to London with the whale oil
brought in from these voyages, returning with hemp,
hardware and similar products of the old world to sell in
the new.

On December 31, 1754, William Rotch married Elizabeth Barney. He made another equally important choice
after his return to the island: he joined Nantucket's Society of Friends.

We shall look more closely at Nantucket's Quakers in
another chapter. Quakerism, it happened, underwent a
sea change on its journey to the island. Nantucket Quakers were a pragmatic group but they abided by Quaker
principles nonetheless, if occasionally adapting religious
tenets to changing circumstances. Although William
Rotch was one of Nantucket's most dedicated Quakers,
his faith did not prevent him from making a fortune. Not

only did his Quaker beliefs support and sustain him through the difficult times of the American Revolution, they also helped him save the island from disaster, as we shall see.

Most of the fortune came first. William Rotch was in the midst of, and soon became a central figure in, a great boom in whaling on the island. By the 1770s Nantucket was bringing in and shipping out 26,000 barrels of sperm oil and 4,000 barrels of right whale oil every year. Some sixty-five vessels sailed from Nantucket annually, more than from any other port and almost half as many as from all the ports of the Massachusetts Bay Colony.

Nantucket whalemen were nearly everywhere in the Atlantic. And Nantucket's merchant ships, carrying the whale oil to England, were setting records for transatlantic crossings. Benjamin Franklin, we all learned at school, "discovered" the Gulf Stream. He learned about it because he was nearly a Nantucketer; his mother, Abiah Folger, came from Nantucket. Benjamin Franklin kept in touch with his relatives on the island, and it was through one of them, Captain Timothy Folger, that he was able to get a plotting of the Gulf Stream. When Franklin was in London as an American emissary, he was asked by English merchants why it was that their ships took as much as two weeks longer to reach America than it took some of the American ships. Franklin discovered that Captain Folger was also in London and turned to him. Folger explained that it was really quite simple: there existed a "broad river," the Gulf Stream, in the North Atlantic, running eastward; Nantucket whalemen had long ago discovered it when they crossed it sailing south after the sperm whale. Folger provided a map

charting the course of the Gulf Stream, and could not
resist pointing out that on many occasions "we have
informed them [the British] that they were stemming a
current that was against them to the value of three miles
an hour and advised them to cross it, but they were too
wise to be counselled by simple American fishermen."
Franklin presented Captain Folger's sketch, which is little different from today's charts of the stream, to the
British merchants, along with directions on how to avoid
it; but the British captains scoffed and continued to sail
the same course against the flow of the Gulf Stream,
losing two weeks of time on all their westward voyages.

One of the most eloquent—and most often quoted—
tributes to the Nantucket whalemen was made by a
Briton, Edmund Burke. This too was evidently inspired
by Benjamin Franklin. On March 22, 1795, two days after
he had spent several hours with America's emissary before Franklin's departure for home, Burke rose in the
House of Commons to speak of the Nantucketers.

"Consider," he said, "the wealth which they have
drawn from the seas by their fisheries. The spirit in which
that enterprising employment has been exercised ought
to raise your esteem and admiration. Pray, sir, what in
the world is equal to it? Pass by the other parts and look
at the manner in which the people of New England have
of late carried on the whale fishery. Whilst we follow
them among the tumbling mountains of ice, and behold
them penetrating into the deepest frozen recesses of
Hudson's Bay and Davis Straits, whilst we are looking for
them beneath the Arctic Circle, we hear that they have
pierced into the opposite region of polar cold—that they
are at the Antipodes, and engaged under the frozen ser-
pent of the South; the Falkland Islands, which seem too

remote and romantic an object for the grasp of national ambition, is but a stage and resting place in the progress of their victorious industry."

Edmund Burke's flowery eloquence had a purpose, which was to sway Parliament from voting for a bill to curtail New England fishing rights. He failed, and England took one more repressive step on the course that would lead to war.

William Rotch, and his brother Francis in Boston, were provided with dramatic and expensive proof of this course. And that is why the building at the foot of the square carries the names "Dartmouth, Beaver, Eleanor."

In 1772 William Rotch had contracted with Nantucket's town fathers to build his warehouse. It was constructed by Rotch for the town, and the first two floors of the building were to be offices of the town. Rotch was to have the third floor and the attic, for which he cannily designed the gambrel roof.

On the building today is the date 1772, but it was not completed until 1774. At about that time two Rotch ships cleared from London for Boston. One was the *Dartmouth*, owned by Francis Rotch, William's brother, and named for the town on the Acushnet River where their father had built his shipyard and expanded into what was now called Bedford. The other ship was the *Beaver*, chartered to William. Both ships had carried whale oil to London and were now returning to the American colonies with a cargo of tea.

The rest is history so colored by legend that we might consider again what actually happened at the so-called Boston Tea Party, at least from the Rotches' vantage point.

On Sunday, November 28, 1773, the *Dartmouth* came

into Boston Harbor followed by the *Beaver* and a third tea-laden ship, the *Eleanor,* owned by another shipper. The captains were ordered to tie up at Griffin's Wharf.

Francis Rotch was in Boston, well aware of the Bostonians' angry boycott of tea in response to London's new tax on the colonists' favorite beverage. So he was not so surprised as he was concerned when told by a group of Patriots that he would unload his ship "on his peril." If he knew what was good for him, they warned, he would send the ship back to London. To make sure that the tea was not unloaded surreptitiously, a band of twenty-five armed men—one of them named Paul Revere—stood watch.

The holds of the *Dartmouth, Beaver* and *Eleanor* had 342 chests of tea valued at £18,000. And Francis Rotch knew that Boston Port regulations stipulated that if the tea were not unloaded within twenty days of arrival it would be confiscated by the British authorities. He concluded that he had no choice but to send the ships back.

But the Rotches found themselves neatly trapped between the two sides in the tea controversy. In response to the Bostonians' boycott, Governor Thomas Hutchinson ordered His Majesty's soldiers on Castle Island, overlooking the harbor entrance, to fire on any ship attempting to leave Boston with its cargo of tea. On issuing his order Governor Hutchinson departed for his estate in Milton, 14 miles south of Boston.

For more than two weeks, while the ships sat at Griffin's Wharf, Francis Rotch tried to work out some sort of compromise. If he could not unload the tea he would lose it all; but the Bostonians held firm. The alternative was to make a run for it, under the cannon of

Castle Island; Francis Rotch knew that would be suicidal.

With only four of the twenty days to go, Rotch and nine Bostonians, led by Samuel Adams, appeared before the Collector of the Port and demanded special clearance to take the ships out of the harbor. To his surprise Rotch was told to come back in three days. But when he did he was told that the clearance had been denied.

Rotch had one day left, and he used it to go out to Milton and confront Governor Hutchinson. The governor refused to clear the ships. Confiscation would be authorized the next day. And by the time Rotch had returned to Boston, the city's Patriots had decided to act on their own.

It was far from the secret, stealthy act of American legend. Thousands of Bostonians gathered on the shore to watch. The 150 men who went aboard the ships had blackened their faces to discourage recognition; some, but not all, disguised themselves as Indians. They worked quietly and methodically through the late hours of December 16, boarding the *Dartmouth* first, then the *Beaver* and last the *Eleanor.* The tea was brought on deck; the boxes were broken open and dumped into the ebbing tide of Boston Harbor. There was no rioting or carousing. The only damage done was to a door lock on one of the Rotch ships; it was carefully repaired. Francis Rotch later said that someone had proposed to John Hancock that the ships and the tea should be burned, but that Hancock "opposed any such proceedings."

News of the loss reached William Rotch on Nantucket not long before much graver news came from London. His Majesty's Government responded to the Boston Tea Party by closing all New England ports. No American

vessels would be permitted in or out of any harbor along
the coast. The decree included the islands as well. This
was a far harsher retaliation for the islanders. Boston
could be supplied overland; Nantucket could not.

Nantucketers reacted the only way they could. They
ignored the order and slipped in and out of Nantucket's
harbor, which was not immediately blockaded, past the
ships lying in watch off Boston and the other mainland
ports.

This may have presented a personal dilemma to William Rotch; but if it did, he did not reveal it. William
Rotch was a sincere Quaker. He once claimed that it
would be fair to say of him that he "busied himself on
two continents while thinking all the time of the life
hereafter." He also said that he was never satisfied with
his adherence to Quaker principles, and in fact never
satisfied with himself. No doubt his Quaker conscience
might have been less disturbed if he had not found himself in the nearly impossible situation that was now de-
veloping on Nantucket.

The situation was precipitated on the mainland. The
Boston Tea Party, the torch-lit mob scenes, even the
Boston Massacre, were merely manifestations of the ir-
reconcilable conflict and the war that was sure to come.
When it did come, the news of the bloodshed at Lexington and Concord reached Nantucket two days after the
battles. And William Rotch, like every Nantucketer, knew
that all of them on the island were caught in a crossfire.
As Patriots they would be easy, open targets for the
British: one man-of-war could round up in the harbor
and level the town. But as Tories they would be equally
open to destruction by the Continental Army and Navy,

even the pitiful Navy the colonies had formed in the early months of the Revolution.

If they needed it, the Nantucketers could look to the example of the people on the neighboring island of Martha's Vineyard. The Vineyarders took an active part in the early stages of the war, organizing companies of Continental soldiers and sending privateers out to harass British shipping. The British reaction was a ruinous raid in September 1778, and the Continental mainland forces could do nothing to aid in the island's defense. Most Vineyarders ceased their warmaking, and one Vineyard historian wrote that "now no one would suspect a war was going on."

For William Rotch on Nantucket there was a third concern. As a Quaker he was a pacifist. In the years of war that followed he remained a pacifist. On some occasions he was forced to trim his sails to the wind, as a Nantucketer would say. Yet William Rotch's Quakerism was probably the single most important factor in the island's narrow escape from annihilation in the American Revolution.

Pacifism was an article of faith to many Nantucketers; it was the only alternative for the others. But pacifism carries a heavy price: it requires neutrality. Whatever one's sympathies or beliefs, one cannot fight for them, or support the fight for them. The usual result is contempt from both sides. In the case of Nantucket's Quaker pacifists, they were simply accused of being Tories.

There was some reason for this. Nantucket had a very good business going with London, which was buying nearly all the whale oil the island could produce. Moreover, there were a great many Tories on the island; in fact, when the war started Tory refugees streamed to the island. Many of them, for some reason, thought they could more easily get to London from Nantucket. Others seemed to think that the island was some sort of Tory refuge. One refugee from the Boston area was William Vassal; his mother was a Nantucket Gardner, and his home in Cambridge had been requisitioned for General George Washington's headquarters. There were a few Patriots, too. One was John Pulling, who had his own good reasons for fleeing Boston: he had lit the lanterns in the Old North Church Tower to signal Paul Revere. Pulling arrived on a fishing boat and stayed on the island until the British were driven from Boston some months later. While refugees from the mainland came to Nantucket, some islanders, especially those with strong sympathy for the Patriots' cause, packed up and moved to the mainland.

It was perhaps understandable under the circumstances that the embattled delegates in Philadelphia were unsympathetic to the Nantucketers' problems. However impressed they may have been by Nantucket's plight, they were suspicious of the islanders' allegiance. As important as any consideration for the Nantucketers was the necessity to keep colonial provisions from benefiting the British forces. Who knew what proportion of any supplies to Nantucket would remain on the island, and how much would be passed on to the British by the island's Tories? One of the more suspicious Americans was General Washington, who referred to the Nantucketers as "unfriendly and notoriously disaffected to the cause of American liberty."

So it was not much more surprising to the Continental

Congress than it was to the islanders when Nantucket officially tried to proclaim its neutrality. To most Nantucketers at the mercy of the warring forces it was a realistic and logical move. But to Philadelphia it merely confirmed earlier suspicions that the island was a hotbed of Tories.

That too may have been a logical assumption under the circumstances. It has always been difficult for a committed man to understand and accept the position of the uncommitted man, and this seems especially true of Americans. If in the full confidence of 20th-century America we must assume that anyone who does not agree with us must be against us, how much more persuasive this simplistic reaction must have been in Philadelphia in 1776. The petition for neutrality was greeted with derision.

But what it meant on Nantucket during the American Revolution was that instead of being regarded as no one's enemy, the islanders were regarded as everyone's enemy. And they were not long in finding out.

On May 23, 1775, little more than a month after the opening guns of Lexington and Concord, Nantucket had its first visitation. It had rained in the morning, and a sharp northwesterly had cleared the skies when sails appeared off the north shore. The little fleet tacked into the harbor and dropped anchor. Boats rowed to the wharf.

It was all very military, considering the newness of the Continental Army. Drums rattled, fifes shrilled and Continental flags whipped in the wind as a hundred soldiers marched up the wharf, trying to keep in step. Their commander announced that they had come after some flour that the Nantucketers intended to smuggle to General

Gage in Boston. No one on the island knew what the Continental officer was talking about. Most suspected the visitors of enjoying an excuse for an outing on the island. The soldiers stayed four days, not searching painstakingly for the flour but marching back and forth on the hills behind the town, helping themselves to items in the local stores and drinking in the taverns. When they left they took a few provisions and—much more important to Nantucket—fifty whaleboats.

It was the first of many such incursions from both sides, and this one served to confirm the sympathies of Nantucket's Tories. One of them was the spirited young Kezia Coffin, of whom we shall see more in a future chapter. In her diary Kezia referred to the visitors as "rebel low-lived fellows" and "sons of Balaal." A confirmed Tory, Kezia spoke for many of Nantucket's other Tories when she commented on the Declaration of Independence: "Horrible! I wish they and all their well-wishers had been strung fifty feet in the air before they had been suffered so far to bring about their wicked and ruinous plans. I believe the only motive they have in view is to aggrandize themselves, they ache not for their bleeding country; the Lord reward them according to their works."

The Lord, it happened, did. But from the perspective of Nantucket at the time, it was difficult for many to see the rebels' cause in a kindly light.

Nantucket was not allowed, of course, to proclaim its neutrality. Petitions to Philadelphia were denied, for obvious reasons. There were other sections of the colonies where Nantucket's example might be seized upon as an excuse for something less than an all-out effort, particularly during the more difficult and disheartening phases of the war. As for the British, His Majesty's naval vessels blockaded the island from time to time, and British privateers occasionally sat off the harbor entrance, picking off any Nantucket vessel attempting to go in or out. But a major harassment came from a group of Tories called "Refugees."

These were mainland Loyalists, most of whom were in fact refugees: they had been driven from their homes by the Patriots and had formed a ragtag guerrilla army under British auspices. Their specialty seemed to be raids upon defenseless communities. Nantucket was one of their favorite targets.

On April 5, 1779, a band of Refugees, under the leadership of one George Leonard, swooped down on Nantucket. The raiders arrived in seven vessels and swarmed through the town, helping themselves to what food and drink they could find. Guards were posted about the town and Nantucketers were ordered to stay in their houses. After an uneasy night, the townspeople defied the raiders and assembled near the wharves, where they found Leonard and his men looting the stores and warehouses. From Thomas Jenkins' warehouse came 260 barrels of whale oil, as well as coffee, tobacco and other stores. The raiders started to load their loot on their vessels. The watching islanders began to gather in groups and talk about a counterattack.

It was a moment of anguish and decision for Nantucket's Quaker leaders. Clearly some of the islanders were ready to fight. They had risked their lives to bring supplies through the blockades and they were not going to stand by while these men robbed them.

William Rotch sympathized with his fellow Nantucketers. But more than that, he feared open conflict. Nantucket had avoided armed battle so far. An attack on the Refugees could precipitate fiery British retaliation against the island.

Rotch moved quickly. With two other Friends he pushed through the crowd and tried to reach George Leonard, leader of the raiders. They were met by a guard with a bayonet. Leonard, the guard informed them, had already gone out to one of the ships anchored outside the harbor entrance.

Rotch managed to talk his way past the guard and to persuade one of the Refugees to take him out to Leonard's ship. The three Quakers left the wharf, cautioning their fellow Nantucketers to be patient until they returned.

They were gone some time. When they returned Leonard was with them, accompanied by some of his lieutenants. Rotch and the two other Quakers, with Leonard and his men, walked through the muttering crowd to Rotch's warehouse. They disappeared inside and did not come out for more than an hour.

In the meeting room of his warehouse Rotch warned Leonard that he was risking bloodshed, in which he was sure to lose some of his men. The Nantucketers, he said, "would not bear it much longer." He also hinted at a possibility that must have been on Leonard's mind: there had been reports of a Patriot expedition from Boston. If the Bostonians found the Refugees here, there would be a slaughter.

Leonard was sufficiently impressed to agree to leave at once. He and his men came out of Rotch's warehouse and ordered the raiders to assemble for departure. Then, as they were leaving, five of the Refugees seized a Nantucket brigantine. Angry Nantucketers threatened to storm the vessel and take it back. Rotch urged them not to. The Nantucketers argued that there were only five raiders aboard and that the brigantine could easily be retaken. Rotch pointed to the guns aboard the Refugees' other vessels, and offered to pay for the brigantine himself if they would let it go. The Nantucketers sullenly watched the raiders leave, with their plunder and the brigantine but without further looting.

Still, for Leonard and his men, it was such easy picking that they promptly planned another raid. Word of it reached Nantucket. A town meeting called on Rotch, Benjamin Tupper and Samuel Starbuck to go to Newport, the nearest headquarters of the British fleet, and present a "memorial," stating Nantucket's case and pleading for the British naval authorities to call off Leonard and his men. The three envoys set sail in the sloop *Speedwell.* En route they were halted by a Continental vessel. Rotch explained his mission and showed the American captain the memorial. The captain had it copied and let the Nantucketers proceed.

Newport Harbor was full of ships arming for raids along the coast. Rotch and his companions were at first told to leave. But when they announced that they would stay until someone gave them a hearing, they were finally permitted to make their case before the Board of Refugees. George Leonard, leader of the first raid, was there; he made an angry argument against sparing Nantucket. But the arguments of Rotch, Tupper and Starbuck were at least convincing enough for the Newport authorities to send them on to New York. There they presented their memorial to Commodore Sir George Collier.

The Commodore received them aboard the warship *Raisonable* in New York Harbor on June 23, 1779. He listened to their case, read their memorial and declared that the raids would be called off.

Rotch quickly seized the opportunity to ask another favor. He pointed out that there had recently been an exchange of prisoners. Nantucket, having taken no part in the fighting, despite such provocations as the one they had just described, had no British prisoners to exchange. But many Nantucketers captured as their ships tried to leave or return to the island were still aboard British prison ships. Could the commodore consider releasing these men? The commodore could. The meeting, Rotch wrote later with Quaker understatement, "was a great relief."

The envoys returned to find that trouble threatened from the other side. Seeing the copy of their memorial made by the American captain who had halted them on their way to Newport, General Horatio Gates complained to the Massachusetts General Court that the Nantucketers were treating with the enemy. The town was ordered to present its defense to the General Court, which it did. The Court could find no proof of treason, but ordered that no such missions be sent to the British in the future.

Yet William Rotch's duties as a diplomat were not finished. Despite the promise by Commodore Collier, more Refugees swooped down on the island, capturing fishing vessels and looting the wharves. And despite the order from the General Court, the townspeople voted to send another delegation to plead with the new British naval commander, Rear Admiral Robert Digby.

Rotch asked to be excused from this mission. He explained that he had been "confined nearly nine months with the Rheumatism, had just left my crutches and was hobbling about with a cane." But the other members of the delegation, Samuel Starbuck of the first mission and Benjamin Hussey, refused to go without him. "At last I consented," Rotch later wrote, "under great apprehension that I should not live to return."

It was a difficult and painful voyage. Off Rhode Island the seas were so heavy and the pitching of the ship so great that Rotch could scarcely bear it; to relieve his agony they anchored in the lee of Long Island until the wind moderated, then continued to New York.

They were received by one Commodore Affleck, who quickly announced that he had no intention of helping them, and for what he considered sufficient reason. The British had granted the Nantucketers a few special permits for whaling expeditions. Now, Affleck claimed, those permits were being used by mainlanders, who must have bought them from the Nantucketers. Affleck quoted a British captain in Boston who "told me that you could hardly find a vessel but what had the permits."

To Starbuck and Hussey it evidently seemed like the end of a useless mission. Rotch, however, recalled: "I heard him patiently through while he was giving us such a lecture." Then he said, "Commodore Affleck, thou hast been greatly imposed on in this matter. . . . Those permits were put into my hands. I delivered them, taking receipts for each, to be returned to me at the end of the voyage, and an obligation that no transfer should be made nor copies given. I received back all the permits except two, before I left home, and should probably have received those two on the day that I sailed. Now, if any duplicity has been practiced, I am the person who is accountable, and I am here to take the punishment that such duplicity deserves."

Commodore Affleck studied the stern Quaker figure confronting him and said, "You deserve favor. I am going to the Admiral. Do you be there in an hour." They were, and the admiral granted their request: an order would be issued forbidding all Refugee raids on the island of Nantucket. "Thus after a storm," Rotch wrote, "came a pleasant calm." Again seizing the opportunity, Rotch asked for more whaling permits; he got twenty-four. He "returned home," he wrote, "much improved in my health."

Still Nantucket's man of peace could not escape other confrontations of war. On March 27, 1782, a dozen Nantucket Friends set out for the Quarterly Quaker Meeting at Sandwich, on Cape Cod. The danger of capture on the open waters was not enough to deter the Quakers from their Quarterly Meeting. The vessel was Rotch's, and he was one of a dozen people aboard; ten were men, two were women.

Off Gay Head they were overtaken by a British privateer, robbed and ordered into a small boat. Rotch led the others aboard the privateer to see if he could talk the privateersmen into letting him keep his vessel. He knew that on some privateers decisions were made by a vote of the crew. That seemed to be the case aboard this ship. "I pleaded earnestly," Rotch said later, "and sometimes nearly obtained a majority to give her to us. But another can of grog would be stirred up by those who would not consent to release her, and this never failed to gain several to their side." Finally the Quakers were ordered into the small boat. Rotch refused, continuing to argue that his vessel should be returned to him. Then the captain "sent a furious fellow to drive us off." The sailor came at them with a cutlass held high and shouted, "Be gone with the boat, or I'll cut your heads off." Rotch later described the scene. "I looked him earnestly in the face, eye to eye, and with a pretty stern accent said, 'I am not afraid of thy cutting my head off. We are prisoners. Treat us as such, and not talk of cutting our heads off.' " The man lowered the cutlass, Rotch recounted, "and seemed much struck by my boldness."

The defiant Quaker and his companions were still standing on the privateer's deck when two American vessels came on the scene. The British privateers scrambled into a boat and rowed for shore, pursued by the Americans. All but one were caught—the one, Rotch noted, "who had threatened to cut off our heads." The Americans returned Rotch's vessel and belongings to him and his friends—after collecting a salvage fee, which Rotch gladly paid.

A brave and spirited man, a man of God who felt keenly the hardships of his fellow Nantucketers during the years of war. Rotch also realized that his neutral stand was not popular with everyone. Later, in his autobiography, he wrote: "The people who thought we ought to have joined in the War (not Friends) began to chide and murmur against me. They considered me the principal cause that we did not unite in the War (which

I knew was immeasureably the case), when we might
have been plentifully supplied, but were now likely to
starve; little considering that if we had taken part, there
was nothing but supernatural aid that could have prevented our destruction."

Gradually the siege strangled the island. Provisions
ran out. The soil, as always, was too poor to grow enough
produce for everyone. The winters were particularly
harsh; as so often happens amidst other misfortunes, the
weather turned bad. In January 1870 the harbor was
frozen over and Nantucketers walked across to Coatue
and chopped down every tree and shrub in sight. They
used the wood, along with peat dug from the boggy low
places of the island, for their feeble fires. And as they
huddled in their houses they could hear the sheep bleat-
ing and brushing against the houses for warmth. Nantucket's hardy sheep that had survived for more than one
hundred winters on the island were devastated by the
winters during the war. When they huddled together on
the moors, the ice storms drove them over the cliffs, to
die in the surf on the beach. Others succumbed to expo-
sure and starvation when snow covered the island. There
were ten thousand sheep on the island when the Revolutionary War started; half were gone when it was over.

The years and the war were even harder on Nantucket's other means of livelihood, her fleet of ships. The
few permits that men like Rotch could wangle from the
British did little to help. Whaleships went out only to be
captured by American privateers, whose captains considered British permits as evidence that the whalers were in
league with the enemy. The Massachusetts General
Court was also persuaded to authorize some whaling

voyages out of Nantucket; but permits had to be obtained at Falmouth, and British captains regarded a Nantucket whaleship with an American permit as fair game. Moreover, the bluff-bowed whaleship was an easy mark for the swift privateers of both sides. Some Nantucketers successfully completed voyages to the South Atlantic and returned with full holds, only to be captured as they waited for the tide to lift them over the bar into the harbor. When a few barrels of oil were safely brought home, they would frequently be captured as soon as another Nantucket ship loaded them and tried to make it to a foreign port. By the end of the war 12,467 tons of Nantucket's 14,867 tons of shipping were lost. The personal losses were even greater. When the war at last ended, a third of Nantucket's population had been killed; out of 500 families, there were 202 widows and 342 orphans.

But the end of the war meant that Nantucket could start all over to rebuild the whaling fleet that had been so promising a decade earlier. William Rotch was ready. The war had cost him financially, too, probably more than any single Nantucketer. His losses, amounting to $60,000, would be more than the equivalent of $1 million today. He now tried to recoup. In December 1782, hearing a rumor that peace was about to come, he sent off two ships to London. They were the *Bedford* and the *Industry,* just returned from the Brazil Grounds laden with sperm oil. The *Bedford* arrived off the Downs in the first week of February and went up the Thames. On February 6, 1783, she anchored near the Tower of London. The Treaty of Paris, ending the war, had not yet been signed. Crowds of Londoners gathered on the

Thames embankment to look at the first ship to fly the American flag in London. The *Industry* arrived a month later.

So William Rotch was back in business, ready to expand the Rotch whaling empire, when the devastating news came from London. The British had lost the military war but were still fighting the economic war. Parliament decreed a tax of £ 18 per barrel on whale oil shipped from the new United States of America.

During the war the British had started their own whaling industry. Their ships had made inroads into the northern whale fishery around Greenland and the Arctic, source of the "black oil" of the Arctic right whale. Now they intended to dominate the southern whale fishery, with its rich sperm whales. The surest way to do that was to discourage the Nantucketers from restoring their whaling fleet. And the surest way to cripple the Nantucketers was to cut off their best market—namely, England. London alone spent £300,000 a year on whale oil for the city's street lamps. Thus the prohibitive tax. At the same time, British whaling merchants offered inducements to Nantucket whalemen to go to England and man their ships.

The Nantucketers tried the only legal maneuver they could think of: once again they petitioned the American Congress for permission to declare their neutrality. Congress was not persuaded. And in any case, the British had no intention of agreeing to any device that would again pit their whalemen against Nantucket whalemen.

So, after virtually leading Nantucket through the war years, William Rotch felt that he had no choice but to desert his island. It was the only way to survive. Other

Nantucketers preceded him to British whaling ports at Milford Haven in Wales, and Dartmouth in Nova Scotia. William Rotch, however, had bigger ideas.

He went to London to propose a transplantation of Nantucket's whaling industry to England. He would lead one hundred Nantucket whalemen and their families to England and set up a Nantucket whaling center in an English port, still to be selected.

Rotch was welcomed by Prime Minister William Pitt. But the prime minister passed him along to Charles Jenkinson, the shrewd president of England's Board of Trade. Jenkinson had ideas of his own. Better to attract Nantucketers to British ships, he reasoned, than to establish a Nantucket-in-England. Jenkinson responded to Rotch's proposal with a masterful use of the bureaucratic technique: delay. For nearly five months Rotch waited for an answer to his proposition. Finally he concluded that there was no future for his plan in England.

He went to France, where a Frenchman aptly named François Coffyn had been entreating the Nantucketers to help his countrymen compete with the British in the southern whale fishery. In one meeting with French authorities Rotch had an agreement to set up a little Nantucket in Dunkirk, France.

Rotch returned to London to settle some business and found a message from George Rose, Secretary of the Treasury. Rose received Rotch cordially; it appeared that Prime Minister Pitt and some of his ministers were concerned about the potential competition from France. In fact, Rose said, "I am authorized by Mr. Pitt to tell you that you shall make your own terms." Rotch recalled: "I told him it was too late," explaining that he had taken his proposal to France and had made an agreement. "This was affected in five hours," he could not resist pointing out, "when I waited to be called by your privy Council more than five months."

The whaling venture in Dunkirk was beginning to bring its returns when France became torn by dissension, revolt and finally the French Revolution and the Reign of Terror. Rotch, it happened, had just left for England on business when, on January 21, 1793, Louis XVI was beheaded. The French Republic declared war on England. The whaling enterprise at Dunkirk was jeopardized, and William Rotch and the other Nantucketers left France to join those in England.

But William Rotch found that England was not for him. In September 1794 he returned to Nantucket. There the islanders were still struggling to rebuild their whaling industry, and many of them showed their resentment over what they regarded as his desertion. Rotch was upset by the criticism. He went to the settlement his father had created, now called New Bedford, to live out his remaining years, watching the American whaling industry revive and flourish. Nantucket became an even greater whaling port than it had been before, as we shall see in the next chapter. But, as we shall also see, a sandbar inexorably ended Nantucket's supremacy. New Bedford became the new whaling center. And there William Rotch still played a part, although a less vigorous one. A fellow New Bedford resident described him as he neared his ninetieth birthday: "A courtly, venerable looking gentleman . . . tall with long, silvery locks, his dress of the true William Penn order—a drab beaver, drab suit, long coat and waist coat, knee breeches with silver buckles. His step is a little faltering but still graceful, as befitting one who stood before ministers and kings in the Old World . . . and in the old Friends' Meeting House on Spring Street, seated in the high seats at the 'head of the meeting,' his very presence is calculated to insure a respect for the principles of peace he so truly inculcated both by precept and example."

Rotch died at ninety-four in his house on William Street. Back on Nantucket Island his warehouse served as the island's Custom House for more than a century, and then as headquarters of the Pacific Club. Members of the Pacific Club were Nantucketers who had sailed to the Pacific Ocean in pursuit of the sperm whale. Thus the old building played a part in the regeneration of Nantucket whaling, as the old man had not.

YOU can stand in front of William Rotch's Counting-house at the foot of Nantucket's square and look past the traffic thumping over the cobblestones to the Pacific Bank at the head of the square. It might be said that Nantucket's fortunes moved up the square from the

126

7
THE GOLDEN AGE

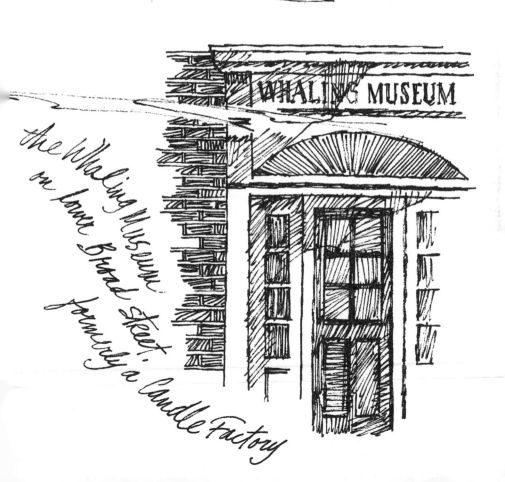

the Whaling Museum on lower Broad Street; formerly a Candle Factory

wharves and the Rotch building to the Pacific Bank, then on up Main Street to the mansions built by whale oil. But first let us turn right and go down South Water Street to Broad Street, where at the head of Steamboat Wharf is a building in which we can see what whaling was really like.

The Whaling Museum was once a candle factory, in which the spermaceti brought back in the whaleships was converted into candles that were sold, and prized, throughout the world. Today the Whaling Museum is filled with evidence and artifacts of the once-great industry. If you are as fortunate as I was on my last visit there, you can hear a man named Adam ("Bud") Craig give a half-hour talk summarizing whaling as it was known to Nantucket. He has a gift for bringing it all alive, even though the whole thing seems absolutely preposterous.

The proof is there, though. Taking up an entire corner of the museum is the jawbone of one sperm whale; it rises two stories to the ceiling. Bud Craig points out that the sperm whale the Nantucketers pursued was the size of three or four Greyhound buses. And the Nantucketers attacked this monster in a whaleboat less than twice the size of a canoe—the whale's tail was larger. Their weapon, the harpoon, was a drumstick compared to the size of the quarry. It was like attacking King Kong with a switchblade knife.

Consider this whale. It is one of the largest creatures on the earth or in the sea. It can plunge to depths that would crush a submarine, and rocket to the surface with such speed that nearly all of its enormous bulk leaves the water. The sound of whales splashing can be heard at a greater distance than they can be seen. One crunch of its massive jaws could reduce a whaleboat to splinters, and a whip of its huge fantail could send the men and their boat flying through the air.

Yet the sperm whale is essentially a docile creature, content to slosh about its own business, diving to search for its favorite food, the giant squid, and surfacing to catch its breath, since it is not a fish but a seagoing mammal. When it expels the breath it has held beneath the sea, sometimes for hours, the air condenses and forms a geyser as high as 20 feet. That was what brought the cry from the masthead of every Nantucket ship: "Blows! Thar she bloooows!"

Bud Craig tells it with stirring verisimilitude, accompanied by all the implements. But even without his help you can visualize it from the evocative assemblage of harpoons, lances, cutting spades and even a complete whaleboat in Nantucket's Whaling Museum. The man who cried out his discovery had been perched for hours in the "crow's nest" atop one of the whaleship's masts, searing in the sun and searching the empty Pacific for just this sign of whales. At his signal the men rushed to their stations beside the whaleboats slung out over the whaleship's sides. The whaleboats were lowered on the run, the men scrambled into them, and within minutes they were off in pursuit of their quarry.

There were usually five whaleboats swung on davits, with a couple of spares lashed to the cabin top. But not all of them were used at once; two or three would be the normal complement, with one of the mates in charge of each boat. If there was a breeze they hoisted the tiny sail in the whaleboat. If not, they bent to their oars—five men sending the light craft skimming across the water toward their target.

The sixth man, usually one of the mates, stood in the

stern at the steering oar. The trick was to sneak up into the deadly circle of the whale, the area in which the animal could swing about and smash the boat. The man at the steering oar gave the orders; the oarsmen were forbidden to look over their shoulders as they approached their goal. No one spoke except the man at the stern; he gave his commands in a near whisper.

Often the whale would be "gallied"—frightened—and would dart off with the speed of a salmon, or would suddenly and silently sink out of sight. But if the whalemen were lucky, they would ease alongside the floating mass, its wet, shiny black hide dotted with barnacles and sea lice and its blowhole still belching clouds of foul-smelling vapor. The harpooner's moment had come. He was the man at the bow oar, which he now quietly shipped. Standing with his knee braced in a specially built crotch at the bow, he hefted his 10-foot harpoon, a long wooden handle with an iron shank and sharp tip, and aimed it at the whale.

The preferred spot was just behind the whale's enormous blunt head. The precise moment was when they came within inches of touching the whale and before the whale felt the telltale ripples from the moving boat. That was when the harpooner, putting all his strength into it, flung his weapon into the black wall of blubber ahead of him.

And that was the moment when the man at the steering oar cried out, "Stern All!" The speed and dexterity of the men at the oars in these few seconds made the difference between life and death for the whole crew.

Stung by the harpoon, the whale could "sound," diving straight for the bottom. So deep could it go that the 1,800 feet of line carefully coiled in the whale tub might run out completely, for which circumstances a barrel was attached to the end of the line; the men in the whaleboat would attempt to follow it, if it occasionally bobbed to the surface, and hope for another chance. Or the whale might try another tactic; it might take off on a 15-mile-an-hour dash across the surface of the Pacific, with the whaleboat rushing after it in the famous "Nantucket Sleighride," the men snubbing the line when they could and letting it out when necessary, as if playing a giant trout. Often the line would whir around the loggerhead with such speed that it began to smoke, and the men had to splash water on it to keep it from burning. During this bouncing dash across the water the harpooner would nimbly climb back to the stern to take the steering oar, and the mate would go forward to get ready for the kill. The mate was the veteran, the expert, on whose dexterity and ability everyone depended.

Sometimes, even before the harpooner and mate could switch positions, the whale could put an end to the chase at the very beginning with one thrash of its huge tail, smashing the boat into pieces or lifting it right out of the water. The whale might then turn on its tormentors and take the boat, men and all, into its huge jaws and crunch it like a dog breaking a bone. Wood and bodies would rain into the sea, and each man could only hope that he would escape the giant teeth and float amidst the debris long enough to be picked up by one of the other boats or the ship.

But if the whale obliged them by diving or running, they would hang on by the narrow thread of their whale line, bounding across the waves or, worse, rolling in the sea while waiting for the mammoth body to come hurtling back to the surface, perhaps right underneath them.

A harpooned whale could run for hours, and frequently whaleboats were carried over the horizon and out of sight of the ship. But eventually, if the harpoon held fast and the line did not snap or run out, the exhausted whale would surface and lie there, as if awaiting the decisive stroke from the mate. He now took one of the lances from the bow and poised for another thrust.

The harpoon was designed to hold fast to the whale; the lance was designed to kill it. With the harpoon line snubbed up close, the executioner lifted his razor-sharp lance and drove it into the mountain of flesh alongside him.

For all its size and layers of protective blubber, the sperm whale had one unprotected vital spot just behind its head, where the lance could penetrate its arteries and flood the whale's lungs with its blood. The harpooner knew when the lance had done its work. A whoosh of gore filled the air (the whalemen called this "setting his chimney afire"). The whale went into convulsions, and the whalemen quickly backed off to watch it die.

A dead sperm whale did not sink. But it weighed as much as 20 tons, and even supported by the water it was an enormous dead weight to be hauled by the men at the oars. Haul it they had to, however, for perhaps 20 miles. Occasionally a whaleboat's crew, with their prize finally secured, found themselves out of sight of the ship; and if fog came down, or a storm overtook them, they might never make it back.

If they were lucky they could spend another twelve to twenty hours pulling the heavy carcass across the sea, on into darkness and perhaps the next dawn. And no matter how exhausted they were, the work had only begun.

The black, rolling body was secured alongside the ship. The cutting stage was unslung, and the cutting-in process began. Standing on the slats of the cutting stage, a few feet above the rolling sharks that had already gathered to snap at the carcass, the men worked swiftly to slice the layers of blubber from the whale, peeling the animal like an orange. The layers were pitched onto the deck, where the brick tryworks were already lit. The blubber went into huge pots and was boiled down into oil, which was then ladled into the barrels to be stowed below. The chunks of flesh left from this process were cut into blocks and fed to the fires below the pots; thus the whale was boiled in its own oil.

With the blubber peeled away, the carcass was decapitated. The remains were cut free to feed the sharks, and the huge head was hoisted on deck by block and tackle. Cutting a hole in the head, one man stepped into it and baled out the rich white spermaceti that made the sperm whale the prize worth all this effort.

When the huge cavity was empty the head was tossed overboard, but not before the lower jaw was cut off. By tradition this belonged to the crew, and from the teeth of the whale's jaw came one of America's most intriguing folk arts: scrimshaw. Filing and polishing the tooth, the whaleman would painstakingly chisel a decoration in it, or paint an elaborate scene. From other whalebone he might make a decorated corset stay, or a pie crimper or even a folding yarn-spinner. The task would take months; but one thing the whalemen had was plenty of time.

Sometimes the teeth were nearly all they got for their hours of dangerous work. A "dry skin," an emaciated, ancient or sick whale, could provide scarcely any oil. And yet a sick whale could also be the most rewarding of all. The sperm whale's food, the squid, has a nearly indestructible hornlike beak that can clog the whale's intestine and set up an infection. The substance from the infection, known as ambergris (and pronounced "ambergrease"), was one of the most fortunate finds a whaleman could make. It was used as a base for perfume, and was extremely valuable. The Nantucket whaler *Watchman* in 1858 brought in 800 pounds of it enough to fill four barrels, and collected $10,000 for the ambergris alone. Finding some of this rare substance could make the difference between success and failure for an entire voyage.

That voyage could take up to five years. The reason, of course, is because the sperm whale, the most prized of all whales, was found in great numbers in the Pacific Ocean. Nantucketers did not make this discovery, any more than Nantucketers originated whaling. It was the British ship *Emilia,* under the command of Captain James Shields, which in 1789 rounded Cape Horn, ran up the west coast of South America and found great numbers of sperm whales.

It happened that the first Pacific sperm whale taken by the *Emilia* was harpooned by a Nantucketer, First Mate Archaelus Hammond. And not long after the *Emilia's* discovery, the Pacific was full of Nantucket ships. Nantucket captains charted much of the then-unknown ocean, and in the process discovered more than thirty islands. There is a Starbuck Island, a Gardner Island, a Mitchell Island and many similar mementos of Nantucket throughout the Pacific. One German cartographer referred to the Pacific as American Polynesia. Nantucket would soon have dominated Pacific whaling, as it had Atlantic whaling, if it had not been for another war.

The War of 1812, like the American Revolution, put Nantucket in the same perilous position, in the same noman's-land between the two combatants. Once again the Nantucketers tried to be recognized as neutrals. Once again they failed. And once again the Nantucket whaling fleet was devastated by war. Roughly half of Nantucket's whaling vessels were lost to enemy action. During the War of 1812 soup kitchens were set up for the poor in Nantucket's streets, and children begged from door to door.

But the islanders knew they could recover and start anew; they had done it after the Revolution. Within eight years of the end of the War of 1812 there were more than eighty Nantucket vessels sailing down around Cape Horn, accomplishing the nearly impossible feat of tacking a square-rigged, round-bowed whaleship against the contrary winds and gales and through the ice off the Horn. That was why a whaling voyage in the 19th century was such a lengthy one; it could take half a year just to get to the whaling grounds. Then more whaling grounds were discovered even farther to the west. Captain Frederick Coffin in the *Syren,* out of London, and Captain Joseph Allen in the *Maro,* out of Nantucket, found an area near Japan swarming with sperm whales, and the "Japan Grounds" became the goal for some of the longest voyages. Some whaling captains even stayed in the Pacific after filling the hold with oil; they would put into the Sandwich (now the Hawaiian) Islands, offload their barrels for shipment home and set out across the Pacific for another two or three years.

It is difficult in today's world of jet-speed transportation to imagine the life of a Nantucket whaleman. Captain Benjamin Worth was a whaleman for forty-one years; during that time he spent a total of six years in Nantucket. Logs and journals from the whaleships attest to the dreariness of this life so far from home. One log entry reads: "Nine months out, and 23 Bbls. sperm. Oh, dear." Another: "Let me see. Today Susie is eleven months old. Oh God bless her. . . . Kiss Susie eleven times for me. Good night Sarah."

Communication took as much as a year. There was a "post office" on Charles Island in the Galápagos; it consisted of a box nailed to a tree. Nantucketers like to tell about an exchange of letters in this mailbox.

> Dear Ezra,
> Where did you put the axe?
> Love,
> Martha

The answer reached Nantucket fourteen months later.

> Dear Martha,
> What did you want the axe for?
> Love,
> Ezra

The next letter took a year.

> Dear Ezra,
> Never mind about the axe. What
> did you do with the hammer?
> Love,
> Martha

At home the whalemen's wives lived their own unnatural life, and a matriarchy developed on Nantucket unlike that in almost any other age. We shall look at some of these sturdy, self-reliant women in the next chapter.

The men not only left behind the world they had known, but also found in the Pacific a world that could scarcely have been more of a contrast. The langorous life of the South Seas was stranger than anything they had expected, even after hearing the colorful yarns spun by those who had been there. Pacific island women were unlike any of Nantucket's frosty females, and there was many an understandable liaison, and even an occasional "marriage," between a lonely Nantucketer and a willing native girl.

But there was also danger. "Cannibals" was the generic term Nantucketers applied to nearly all the island people, although cannibalism in the islands was rare and, in any case, a ritual observance rather than a normal practice. Still, one never knew whether an island was inhabited by friendly natives or by screaming blue-black savages intent on murdering anyone who approached them. And there were islanders who lured white visitors ashore and overwhelmed them with hospitality, only to slaughter them when they were off guard and then loot their ship. Nantucketers who had been brought up among the friendly and honorable Indians of their Massachusetts island were quite unprepared for the moral values of the Pacific islanders, to most of whom treachery seemed to be a meaningless word; so far as the Nantucketers could tell, expediency was the moral code of the South Seas.

Still, as always, there were a few exceptions. There were Pacific islanders who learned from experience that

it was in their best interests to deal fairly with the whalemen, especially on the larger islands most frequented by
the whalemen. There was one whaleman, David Whip-
pey, who became a local chief and stayed with his
adopted people on his own island of Ovalu for the rest
of his life. He was the benefactor, and rescuer, of many
an American shipwrecked near his island.

For most of Nantucket's whalemen, most of the time,
it was a grueling, agonizingly lonely existence, and a
filthy, stinking one as well. Herman Melville, who was a
whaleman in the Pacific himself, wrote that he could nose
a "spouter," as the whaleships were called, a couple of
miles away. "It smelled," he wrote, "like the left wing on
the day of judgment." After reading his classic *Moby Dick*,
read also his *Typee*, and especially *Omoo*, for an authentic
portrayal of life in an extraordinarily different world.

But if the Nantucketers found a weird and wonderful
world across the seas, they brought much of it home with
them, and in the process the little island town was transformed. What we often overlook when we consider Nantucket through the ages is that the island's modern history can almost be subdivided into distinct periods, as its
ancient history can be divided into the periods of the Ice
Age and the Paleo, Early Archaic, Late Archaic and
Woodland Cultures. It could in fact be said that modern
Nantucket has had Early Settler, Early Whaling, Golden
Age and Tourist cultures. And quite different was one
from the other. Look at the Coffin House, the plain
houses snuggled up to the street and the Rotch Countinghouse—and contrast them with the Pacific Bank and
the mansions on Main Street. You can see what a difference there was between Nantucket's Early Whaling and

Golden Age Cultures. Nantucket, in short, was not always the grand showplace that we see in these mansions. The opulent era that they reflect lasted little more than a decade, a few minutes in the recorded time of the island's history. But while it was a short period it was certainly colorful, and it is barely hinted at in the architecture, the gardens and the exhibits in Nantucket's museums.

In 1842, the zenith of Nantucket's prosperity, the island's whaling merchants had eighty-six ships and barks roaming the seas, plus two brigs and two schooners, with a combined capacity of 36,000 tons. Nearly half of all the whaleships in the world sailed from Nantucket. Try to imagine the activity at the heart of this far-flung business. The wharves swarmed with commerce. Dozens of whaleships were made fast to the docks or anchored in the harbor. The wharf built at the foot of Main Street had been replaced by what is now called Straight Wharf. It was bounded by Old South Wharf, built in the 1760s, and by Commercial Wharf, built in the 1820s. Burdett's Wharf, with a few fishing shacks, stood where Old North does now. And New North Wharf, built mainly for packets, stood to the west; in the late 19th century it was renamed Steamboat Wharf, and it was rebuilt in 1915.

The wharves were crowded with ropewalks, warehouses, cooperages and forges. Wagons and handcarts rumbled from one to the other. There was a clanking brass foundry on the south beach. Other warehouses and countinghouses in the square bustled with activity. In the brick building that is now the Whaling Museum, huge presses were squeezing the waxy spermaceti into clean, odorless, smokeless candles that would bring premium prices throughout America and Europe. At one time there were thirty-five of these candle factories in Nantucket.

The streets were crowded with a mixture of people: Portuguese, Malays and South Sea Islanders (usually referred to as "Kanakas") recruited in distant parts and brought home in Nantucket whalers. The stores sold teas and spices from India, pepper from Cayenne, ornamental chests from China, sandalwood and tapa cloth from the South Seas, china from Canton—most brought back by whaleships that had sailed halfway around the world. And from other ports of call, mostly on ships that had delivered whale oil, sperm candles and whalebone corset stays and buggy whips, came Spanish olives, Sicilian oranges, English walnuts, French wines, West Indian rum and molasses, Leghorn bonnets and Merino shawls.

There were the cobblestones that paved the square, and were later extended up Main Street. They made traffic uncomfortable and incredibly noisy, but they were preferable to the quagmire that the heavy drays had made of the streets after every rain. And there was the melodious bell in the tower of the Unitarian Church.

At first this graceful, towering structure was known as the Second, or South, Congregational Church. The first bell, purchased in 1800, had come from the Boston foundry of Paul Revere; but after a few years it had cracked. Its replacement was bought by Nantucket's Captain Charles Clasby, who had chanced upon it in Lisbon in 1812. It was one of six bells intended for a convent but rejected. On its side was chiseled in Portuguese: "To the good Jesus of the Mountain, the devotees of Lisbon direct their prayers, offering Him one

complete set of six bells, to call the people and adore
Him in the Sanctuary. Made by José Domingos Da Casta
in Lisbon in the year 1810." The bell weighs 1,575
pounds and was brought to Nantucket by another Nantucketer, Captain Thomas Cary. With great difficulty it
was raised to the church bell tower in 1815.

There is a legend that the first bellringer, ordered to
ring the bell for two minutes, counted fifty-two strokes
and gave up; even today the bell is tolled fifty-two times
at 7 A.M., noon and 9 P.M.; in the 19th century the 9 P.M.
ringing was the signal for curfew. You can still hear this
beautiful bell at these hours. Listen for it. And on a day
when you feel strong, ask permission to climb the tower,
admire the bell and take a look at Nantucket from one of
the best vantage points on the island.

Perhaps as you admire the bell and the view of the
mansions below you can appreciate an exchange that
supposedly took place between the parishioners of Nantucket's Church and those of Boston's Old North
Church, whose tower is famous for the lights that sig-
naled Paul Revere. From Old North Church came a letter
to Nantucket's church saying that the Bostonians had
heard of the fame of Nantucket's Lisbon bell, and asking
if the Nantucketers would like to sell it. From Nantucket's church went the answer: the islanders could not
consider selling their bell. But they had heard of the
fame of Boston's Old North Church; would the Bostonians be interested in selling their church?

That was the sort of confident, not to say arrogant,
spirit of Nantucket in the mid-19th century. It was the
acknowledged whaling port of the world and as such was
a place of power and wealth. When Daniel Webster vi-

sited Nantucket for the first time in 1835, he was aston-
ished at the island metropolis, and called it "the unknown city in the ocean." Webster had not realized that
Nantucket's influence was worldwide. Nantucketers
charted the Atlantic and Pacific, influencing not only life
on the Pacific islands but also the market for that valuable commodity, whale oil, as well as the goods for which
whale oil was traded.

But at a price. One day in 1821 the church bell tolled
a signal for assembly. Nantucketers gathered in the
square in front of the Post Office, where the Postmaster
read to them a letter just received.

> Off St. Maria
> Pacific Ocean
> At 5 P.M. spoke and boarded Ship *Dauphin,* Captain Gimri
> Coffin; on board of this ship I heard the most distressing
> narrative that ever came to my knowledge. . . .

This was the first news to reach Nantucket of what was
probably its worst whaling tragedy. On November 20,
1820, the Nantucket whaleship *Essex* was attacked by a
whale near the Equator in mid-Pacific. The blow opened
a hole in the bow of the *Essex* so large that the ship filled
and sank, leaving Captain George Pollard and his crew
of nineteen in three whaleboats. Not until three months
later were two of the boats picked up by passing whaleships. The third boat was never found. Only five men
survived, and to do so they were forced to cannibalism,
drawing lots to pick the crew members who would be
sacrificed for their shipmates.

The full details of this gruesome odyssey were not

revealed until the survivors got home. But even the spare account in the letter to the town was enough to bring tears to the men and women assembled in the square. Many Nantucketers maintained a shameful silence about this tragedy. Years afterward, when asked about it, an islander said, "On Nantucket we do not talk about the *Essex.*"

There were other sinkings, even other ships stove by whales. There were mutinies, shipwrecks on coral reefs and mysterious disappearances that were never solved. When the blue flag signifying the arrival of a ship was hoisted in Nantucket's square, wives and children scrambled to the walks on their roofs to look out across the harbor to the bar. Some sadly climbed down after determining that it was not the ship they waited for. But if it was, the anxiety could be even worse: the ship was in, but how many of her crew had survived?

The whalemen had a saying: "For every barrel of oil, a drop of blood." But while many gave their lives in the Pacific, others made a great deal of money. Most of them were the merchants who sent out the ships. And they quickly learned to enjoy their newfound wealth.

Nantucket's Quakers had scorned such conspicuous consumption. But the golden era of Nantucket whaling proved too tempting for their descendents, as we shall see in Chapter IX. As if in a burst of reaction against Quakerism, Nantucket's newly rich blossomed in ornate silks from the Orient and tailored woolens from England. Outfitted horse-drawn carriages appeared on cobblestoned Main Street. But the most obvious change was in Nantucket's architecture.

Gone was the plain lean-to style, and in its place came

the grand porticoed mansions. It was even true of the business buildings; we have seen the contrast between the Rotch warehouse of 1774 and the Pacific Bank of 1818. But the striking contrast was in the homes that the affluent whaling merchants built for themselves and their families.

Architects were brought from the mainland to design these mansions. There was an ambitious, and expensive, architectural fad in the U.S. at the time, and it was eagerly adopted on Nantucket. The Greek Revival style, with its columns and pilasters and ornate interiors, can especially be seen on Main Street. If you will pay the nominal entrance fee, you can examine the grandest mansion that is open to the public, the Hadwen-Satler House on Main Street. Imported paneling and mantel pieces; hand-carved balustrades; separate chimneys for nearly every fireplace; wallpaper and draperies from Europe. And antiques from the Orient that were priceless even then.

Compare this with the Jethro Coffin House and you will get the idea. The whole style of living had changed. No longer did the family congregate in the kitchen; now there were two or three drawing rooms and a formal dining room. The servants' quarters were more commodious than the finest room in an earlier house. And instead of a bare yard with a well sweep or a few steps down to the street, there were fenced-in front lawns and formal gardens in the rear, planted with flowers, shrubs and trees from England, France and Madeira.

Remember, though, that these were the homes of the wealthy few. The Nantucket whaleship provided an early example of profit-sharing, with the officers and crew paid in shares, called "lays," so that everyone received his proportionate part of a successful voyage, or suffered if it were unsuccessful. Still, the proportions—1/18 for the captain down to 1/120 for a cabin boy—meant that the officers and the owners were the only ones who became rich. A good whaleman rose through the ranks, and there were some who were captains in their twenties and who could retire in their forties. You can see many of their homes on Orange Street, which at one time had more captains' residences than any street in America.

But the houses on Orange Street seem like a transition between earlier and later Nantucket; they are larger and better appointed than the first settlers' homes, but modest compared to the mansions built by the ship owners. The big money was made, as usual, by the entrepreneurs, the merchants who were willing to gamble a large investment in return for a huge return on the investment if his ship had a successful voyage. Multiply this by a dozen ships or more and you can understand why Joseph Starbuck could build the luxurious mansions known as the Three Bricks as presents for his three sons.

It was no surprise to the Nantucketers, accustomed to such a double standard, that during the town's so-called Golden Age there were no public schools. As early as 1642 the Massachusetts Bay Colony had proclaimed that every town with a population of more than fifty should have a public school. Nantucket's town fathers simply ignored the law. There were a number of private schools on the island, for the children of the ship owners, the merchants and the captains. There were special private schools teaching seamen's skills, especially navigation. There were some charity schools—one was open only

during the summer months because its donors would not
pay for heating it in the winter. And there was the Admiral Isaac Coffin School, established with funds donated
by Admiral Sir Isaac Coffin and certified by the Massachusetts legislature only after one of the democratically-
inclined legislators insisted on changing its name from
the Admiral *Sir* Isaac Coffin School. But not until 1827,
and only after long and stubborn campaigning by a newcomer named Samuel Jenks, did Nantucket have a public
school.

The islanders' parsimony in such matters extended to
what seemed the ultimate when the town voted not to
light Nantucket's streets at night. It was more frugal to
sell the sperm oil to other cities. London, for example,
reduced its crime rate by lighting its streets, and by 1780
there were more sperm oil lights on Oxford Row than in
all of Paris. But for Nantucketers curfew was cheaper.

Sperm oil and its by-products—spermaceti candles
and lamps, whalebone, the occasional chunk of ambergris, even scrimshaw—constituted the backbone of Nantucket's economy. It also supported hundreds of related
businesses, from coopering to insurance, sailmaking to
banking. But Nantucket was a one-industry town, and the
islanders imported nearly all their necessities. They grew
some of their food and they still pastured large flocks of
sheep that provided them with wool for their clothing
and mutton for their food. But it was perhaps a sign of
Nantucket's single-minded devotion to whaling that
even the island's annual sheep-shearing became an off-
islanders' event as much as a Nantucketer's wool harvest.

Sheep-shearing was a local celebration, attracting ped-
dlers and hucksters from the mainland. Even the shear-

ing itself was mainly done by experts who came to the island for the occasion. In the 19th century the shearing was done in an area near Miacomet Pond. The event was usually a two- or three-day festival in early June. Boys on horseback herded the sheep to the shearing pens, where the off-island experts waited with their tarpaulins and shears. A good shearer would clip all the fleece from one sheep in nine minutes. The fleece was dumped in carts and driven to a central station near town, where it was weighed, baled and stored. Then the fun began.

The *Inquirer* described it: "The carnival has commenced. The orgies of the mutton-worshippers are beginning to burst forth, and all the wooly world is in an agony of helter-skelterishness." In a grand procession every vehicle that could move went rumbling out over the rutted roads to the shearing pens, where tents were set up for entertainment and feasting. Nantucket ladies offered boiled hams and whole roasted pigs. There were red and blue hard-boiled eggs; oysters and clams; pies, puddings and cakes; spruce beer, lemonade—and, no doubt, stronger drinks for those who knew where to get them. As further indication of the decline of Quakerism, there were tents with floors for dancing, and even tables for crap-shooting. Off-islanders came over to take advantage of the opportunity, with tents and booths offering all sorts of trinkets, novelties and plain junk. It was Nantucket's version of the great American country fair.

It might also have been Nantucket's version of the last glorious days of Rome—certainly not because the islanders' festival could compare with the dissolution and depravity of the Romans, but because the days of Nantucket's own golden age also were numbered. As with

the end of the first settlement on the bay that became
Capaum Pond, the days of prosperity could be measured
in the sands that slowly crept across the harbor mouth.
The same tides and currents along Nantucket's north
shore that had built the sandbar called Coatue and
formed the harbor, the same sands that had closed off
Capaum Pond, were inexorably blocking the entrance to
the harbor and choking off its lifeline.

As the sands built up on the bar at the harbor entrance,
more and more ships were forced to wait for longer
periods to enter and leave the port. At first the ships had
only to anchor outside the bar at low tide. But Nantucket
whaling merchants built and bought from other ship-
yards larger and larger ships. Whalers required deeper
water at the same time that the passage into Nantucket
was becoming shallower.

By the beginning of the 19th century the bar had built
up to the point where there were only 6 to 8 feet of water
at mean low tide; high tide was only 2 to 4 feet deeper
than that. In 1828 the islanders contracted with a dredge
to deepen a channel through the bar. But the channel
filled up in the next storm. There was some discussion
of the practicality of jetties, but it was countered by the
argument that another bar would build up at the jetties'
mouth. By the 1830s the whalers averaged nearly 330
tons, and drew 10 feet or more when fully laden. Several
of the whalers were above 400 tons. Some could cross
the bar at high tide after their cargoes were unloaded
into lighters. Others had to put into Edgartown's deeper
harbor on Martha's Vineyard and ship the oil from there
to Nantucket. It became obvious that this extra expense
would inevitably drive most of Nantucket's whaling mer-

chants to the Vineyard and to New Bedford on the mainland. That was when one Nantucketer came up with an
outlandish solution: if the ships could not ride over the
bar, why not lift them bodily over it?

His name was Peter F. Ewer, and a model of his contraption can be seen in the whaling museum. Ewer called
his device "the Camels," evidently because that was the
name given to a similar mechanism in Holland, where it
had been invented by one M. M. Bakker and used in 1688
to carry ships over two sandbars in the Pampas Passage
of the Zuider Zee near Amsterdam. Essentially the camels amounted to a floating drydock. Two enormous pon-
toons were chained together and floated out to the ship.
Vents were opened and the contraption sank in the
water. The ship was positioned between the two pon-
toons, the chains were snubbed up to cradle the ship's
sides, and steam pumps emptied the water from the pon-
toons. As the drydock rose from the water it lifted the
ship, and the whole assemblage could then be towed
over the bar. The camels were supposed to handle an
800-ton ship, larger than any of Nantucket's whalers at
the time.

The first trial of Ewer's floating drydock was held on
August 22, 1842, with the whaleship *Phoebe,* which was
ready to set out for the Pacific. The camels were eased
under the *Phoebe,* whereupon a plank in one of the pon-
toons burst under the pressure of the inrushing water.
With high tide the next day the camels were tried again;
someone opened the wrong valves, the camels listed and
the *Phoebe* almost tipped over. Once more the *Phoebe*
submitted to the camels' embrace; the chains gave way
and the ship fell through, ripping away some of her cop-

per sheathing. The *Phoebe* went back to the wharf for repairs, and on September 19 eased out over the bar on an exceptionally high tide, without benefit of the camels.

With understandable misgivings, Charles and Henry Coffin agreed to try the camels under their 318-ton whaleship *Constitution*. This time the floating drydock worked perfectly: the *Constitution* was over the bar in forty-five minutes. And when on October 15 the *Peru* hove to off the bar, loaded down with 1,340 barrels of sperm oil, the camels triumphantly brought her in, while the townspeople rang bells and fired guns in celebration.

Many Nantucketers will tell you that the camels were a desperate attempt to save the island's whaling industry, and that they failed. The statistics indicate otherwise, at least for a while. In 1843 the camels carried thirty-three ships over Nantucket's sandbar; the next year eleven ships were brought in and out, and in 1845 the number rose to forty-five. There were doubters even then: Samuel Starbuck wrote: "Over fifty Nantucket people put their money into that crazy idea. . . . You can't have mechanical things here on Nantucket."

In fact, the camels did postpone the end of Nantucket's golden age. But as the whaleships became even larger, the expense mounted. The added costs of shipping whale oil from Nantucket instead of from a mainland port gradually made Nantucket whaling prohibitively expensive. The island's fleet declined. By 1846 there were sixteen whaleships registered in Nantucket, sixty-nine in New Bedford; by 1857 there were four whaleships in Nantucket, ninety-five in New Bedford. The camels brought their last ship, the *Martha*, over the bar on June 8, 1849. Then they were hauled onto the harbor beach and left to break up.

The death knell for Nantucket whaling, and for all whaling until the advent of today's butchering factory ships, came not off Nantucket's sandbar but in a shed in Waltham, Massachusetts, in 1838, when a couple of chemists found a method of deriving kerosene from petroleum. Kerosene would shortly light the lamps of the world, replacing more costly sperm oil.

Some stubborn whaling merchants tried to keep the industry alive, and with occasional success: in 1859, one year after the first refinement of kerosene, Joseph Starbuck's *Three Brothers* came back to the island with 6,000 barrels of oil, the largest ever brought into Nantucket. But only ten years later, on November 16, 1869, the barque *Oak* was the last whaler to sail from Nantucket. She was sold in Panama. One year later the barque *Amy* and the brig *Eunice H. Adams* appeared off the bar to wait for the tide. They were the last two whalers to come home to the onetime capital that was rapidly becoming a deserted village.

IT is a short walk up Broad Street from the Whaling Museum to the corner of Centre Street. During the period described in the two previous chapters, when most of Nantucket's men were away at sea and Nantucket's women were left in charge, this street was better known as Petticoat Row. During most of this period the women on Nantucket outnumbered the men 4 to 1. Many of the

8
THE MATRIARCHY

women managed their husbands' counting houses. Others set up shops to sell the produce brought in by Nantucket's ships. So many of these women's shops were on Centre Street that it got the name Petticoat Row.

None of these little shops remain; they were leveled in the Great Fire of 1846. But the buildings that replaced them are not dissimilar. Today you can walk down Centre Street toward the Pacific Bank and the town square and imagine the beehive of activity during these years—a beehive also, perhaps, in the sense that Nantucket in the 18th and 19th centuries somewhat resembled the hive in which the work of many drones served the purpose of one queen bee.

I will resist the temptation to carry the analogy too far: the worker bees traveling off on their distant missions while the hive at home swarms with those carrying out the routine duties supporting the queen in her hive. But the similarity is intriguing, because while the men of Nantucket went off to the South Atlantic and around Cape Horn on their whaling voyages, the women they left behind were forced to assume responsibilities they never would have known under more normal circumstances.

Nantucket's women were quite up to it. There is a legend that when the very first settlers, the Thomas Macy family, were fighting their way through a storm at sea on their way to the island, Sarah Macy suggested that they turn back. Her husband's response was: "Woman, go below and seek thy god! I fear not the witches on earth nor the devils in hell!" Not only might it be said that this was the first and last example of feminine frailty (Sarah was not yet, of course, a Nantucket woman), but it is also an unreliable account, if only because their vessel was an open boat and there was nowhere below to go.

Whatever the reliability of this Nantucket legend, the historical evidence since 1659 is otherwise. In fact, Nantucket seems to have produced and nurtured as hardy, self-sufficient and enterprising a lot of woman as any in the world, except possibly the Amazon.

One enterprising Nantucket woman we have already seen was Wonoma, the Indian princess who brought peace to the two major tribes of Nantucket. The first white settlement on the island was dominated by the Great Lady, Mary Starbuck. Adviser, counselor and diplomat, Mary Starbuck was also a great deal more. The doyenne of "Parliament House" was the mother of four sons and six daughters. At the age of fifty-six, when most people would be expected to be less adventurous, Mary Starbuck took up a new crusade. She welcomed a visiting Quaker missionary, John Richardson, made her home available for Quaker meetings, became a Quaker herself and has ever since been regarded as the prime mover in bringing to the island the faith that influenced its history for two centuries.

Mary Starbuck was Nantucket's Great Lady with her husband Nathaniel at her side. So it was not separation alone that produced Nantucket's other great ladies. There was something more, perhaps the independent, not to say stubborn and eccentric, spirit characteristic of many people who live on islands. Perhaps it was a tonic in the air. In any case, Nantucket bred a special kind of woman. In his classic *Nantucket: The Faraway Island,* the late William Oliver Stephens wrote, "Indeed, it is probable that no other community in America of the size of

Nantucket has ever given to the country so many extraor-
dinary women." Consider a few of them.

Deborah Chase was a great lady of Nantucket in a
somewhat different sense. Deborah is reputed to have
weighed 350 pounds, and evidently all of it was muscle.
On one occasion she was insulted by a young man weighing a mere 160 pounds, whom she promptly seized and
flung onto a nearby roof. Another instance of her prow-
ess had as its victim an unfortunate young man who had
just been married. In his wedding coat—and perhaps
emboldened by nuptial alcoholic consumption—he presumed to embrace Miss Chase. With a flip of her arm she
sent him into a vat of whale oil. A similarly foolhardy
drayman whom Deborah warned when his wagon
bumped the Chase house was so unwise as to repeat the
offense. Deborah came out and tipped the entire rig
bottom-up in the street. It took a gang of men to right
it.

So we can almost take pity on a young sentry who was
patrolling Nantucket's streets during a Refugee raid on
the town at the beginning of the American Revolution.
These Tory marauders found Nantucket an easy mark—
all, that is, except the young man who confronted Deborah Chase. The raiders had proclaimed a curfew: Nantucketers were to stay inside their homes. But the Chase
kitchen ran out of water, and Deborah set out for the
nearest town pump with a pail in each hand.

The sentry, following his orders, marched up to Deborah, ordered her to halt and presented his bayonet.
Deborah simply swung a bucket in a whirring parabola,
knocked the man senseless and went on her way. On her
return, her buckets full, she stepped over the sentry's

unconscious form, not even deigning to use a bit of her precious water to revive him.

Deborah's brother Reuben served under John Paul Jones in the Revolution. Reuben was a fearless fighter, but Jones might have done better to recruit Deborah.

Maria Mitchell was as formidable a woman intellectually as Deborah Chase was physically. The daughter of William Mitchell, cashier of the Pacific Bank, Maria inherited her father's love of mathematics, but became even more devoted to astronomy, to the extent that her father mounted a telescope atop their little apartment on the upper floor of the bank. On the night of October 1, 1847, after many weeks and months of peering through her telescope, Maria, age twenty-nine, spotted what she thought was a new comet. She went down to the apartment where her parents were giving a party and whispered the news to her father, who followed her up to the little observatory and agreed that she seemed to have made a discovery. He promptly reported it to Harvard, just in time, because two days later an Englishman recorded his discovery of the same comet. Maria got credit for being the first. She became world-famous and was invited to Denmark to be honored by the king, and to England where she received more honors.

When in 1861 a new college named Vassar was founded, Maria Mitchell became its first Professor of Astronomy. She was a popular professor, if only because of her independent island manner. Told by a doctor to drink beer as a tonic, she bellied up to the nearest bar, ordered a bottle to take out, looked about her and, as she recounted, "told the man he should be ashamed of his traffic." When a Vassar student proudly announced that she had a cousin on Nantucket, Maria replied that she had 5,000 cousins on Nantucket. And when what would today be called a male chauvinist expressed surprise that Professor Mitchell had enough stamina for the long night hours required for astronomy, she responded, "Sir, my mother had more night work than astronomy will ever demand of any woman. She brought up eight children."

Maria Mitchell was awarded more degrees and honors than any American woman of her generation. But her favorite recollections were of helping young Nantucket whalemen correct their navigating instruments. She retired from Vassar after twenty-three years and moved to Lynn, Massachusetts, where her father had moved after her mother's death. Maria Mitchell died there in 1889 at the age of seventy-one.

There was Lucretia Mott, a descendant of both Tristram Coffin and Peter Folger. In her eighty-eight years she brought up five children and meanwhile toured America speaking for women's rights. She became the earliest champion of women's suffrage; her face appeared on a U.S. stamp issued in 1948, commemorating the hundredth anniversary of the first women's rights convention in Seneca Falls, New York (the stamp cost 3 cents). She was best described by historian Douglas-Lithgow as the "bright morning star of intellectual freedom in America."

There was Anna Gardner, an abolitionist, teacher of freed slaves in the South after the Civil War, author and poet who lived to be eighty-five. There was Phoebe Ann Armstrong, the first woman pastor in New England, a Lyceum lecturer, poet, abolitionist and champion of social reform, temperance and women's rights who lived to be ninety-one. There was Abiah Folger, Ben Franklin's mother. And there was Kezia Coffin.

As you walk down Centre Street toward Main Street and the square, just before you reach India Street you will see on your right a green lawn. There should be a plaque or some sort of historical marker, because here stood the most controversial building in 18th-century Nantucket. It was once the combined home and store of John and Kezia Coffin. To be more accurate, it was the base of operations for Kezia Coffin, the shrewdest, most hard-headed and ruthless merchant in Nantucket.

Kezia was a Folger, and a third cousin of Ben Franklin. She was born on October 9, 1723. On October 4, 1740, just before her seventeenth birthday, she married John Coffin, a captain in the London trade and fifteen years older than she. Captain Coffin spent much of his time at sea. His bride was already accustomed to this, for her father and brothers had shipped out; in fact, one brother was lost at sea the year of her marriage, and her father and another brother went down with their ship four years later.

Kezia Coffin took over her husband's store and was managing a thriving little business when the American Revolution started. Kezia was a Tory; she had no sympathy with the rebels, as she called them, and she felt free to make a deal with the captain of a British ship blockading Nantucket Sound: she provided fruit, vegetables and meat for the British sailors in return for much needed flour from their vessel's storeroom. Nor did she and her husband, when he returned to the island, think twice about sending Coffin sloops in and out of Nantucket Harbor under the cover of darkness. The British and American authorities called it smuggling; Kezia regarded it as the only way to keep the island supplied with the necessities of life.

What she thereupon did with these necessities did not endear Kezia Coffin to her neighbors. In a seller's market, she charged the highest prices she could get. If many Nantucketers felt a spirit of joint sacrifice because of the war, that spirit was not shared by Kezia Coffin. Those who could not pay her prices, or barter goods she needed, went without. As the island's currency supply dwindled, she accepted mortgages on her neighbors' homes. The Coffin store flourished. John Coffin built a house at Quaise, on one of the harbor's eastern coves, and it became known as Kezia's country estate.

Watching Kezia Coffin profit at what they considered their expense, many Nantucketers spread rumors about her dealings with the enemy. The Patriots on the island were the most vociferous because they felt the most aggrieved. Kezia Coffin was trading regularly with the British, they claimed. Coffin ships were running the British blockade with impunity. And Kezia's country house at Quaise was the collection point for smuggled goods and a rendezvous for secret deals with the enemy. So went the rumors, including a claim that Kezia had had a tunnel dug from her house to the beach, and that the tunnel was jammed with illicit merchandise.

Most of the islanders were Quakers and pacifists, attempting to keep from taking sides in the struggle. But they too became angry with Kezia Coffin as they felt her economic stranglehold. And as she displayed her newfound wealth, the disapproving Quakers cautioned her that she was sinning against their principle of plain-living; finally they read her out of the meeting, the Friends' equivalent of excommunication.

Kezia Coffin responded with disdain. She happily left the Quakers and joined the Presbyterian Church. She flaunted her Toryism. When the Loyalist Refugees descended on the town, looting Nantucketers' warehouses, Kezia entertained them in her home on Centre Street. As the necessities of life became scarcer, she raised her prices. When her neighbors proved unable to pay up on their mortgages, she started foreclosure proceedings.

In 1773 she had invited a young lawyer from Connecticut to settle on Nantucket. His name was Phineas Fanning, and in one of her shrewder deals Kezia gave him lodging in return for his legal services. It quickly developed that Phineas Fanning earned his keep. Not only was he busy nearly full time with Kezia's litigious affairs, but he also helped John Coffin build the house at Quaise.

He received another reward. Kezia and John Coffin had one child, a daughter also named Kezia; evidently considering that it would be good business to have a lawyer in the family as well as in the house, Kezia senior urged Kezia junior to marry Phineas Fanning. There is some question concerning the daughter's eagerness for the marriage, but she consented.

Young Kezia was as ardent a Tory as her mother, and evidently Fanning was a Loyalist too. Daughter Kezia also happened to be one of America's most prolific diarists; she started a daily record on January 1, 1775, when she was sixteen, and kept up a running account of her life and that of her neighbors for forty-five more years. From her diary we have learned many of the details of Nantucket's history during this lengthy period.

From her diary we also learn that the Quakers disapproved of Kezia's marriage to the non-Quaker off-islander. On January 13, 1777, Kezia recorded, a committee from Nantucket's Monthly Meeting of Friends called on the young lady and advised her "not to be courted by a Presbyterian and to consider the matter well before I entered the marriage state." They also, she added, "advised me not to dress so fashionable." Kezia, like her mother, decided against Quakerism. She became Mrs. Phineas Fanning on April 5, 1777, in the home of the Reverend Bezaleel Shaw, a Presbyterian minister. Kezia was seventeen, Phineas twenty-seven. In the twenty-one years of marriage that followed they raised six sons and two daughters.

During most of these years Phineas Fanning was extremely busy with his mother-in-law's lawsuits. She even asked Fanning for some sort of legal delegation of authority from her husband. Fanning suggested a power of attorney. She replied: "Thou make it binding to the uttermost power of words and thou mayst name thy reward."

By this time Phineas Fanning was being rewarded sufficiently to support his new home. Presently he was busier than ever. In 1780 Kezia Coffin, now fifty-six, was formally charged with "high treason."

It was an intriguing case for two reasons: it was largely based on a single incident, and it involved not just Kezia Coffin but such an unlikely partner in crime as William Rotch. The incident was the Refugee raid on Nantucket, the one described in Chapter VI and the one in which Deborah Chase taught a lesson to the unwary sentinel. The charge was brought by one Thomas Jenkins, who had perhaps suffered greater losses than any of the other Nantucketers in the raid: his warehouse was looted, and he was part owner of the sloop the raiders had seized.

Jenkins wanted revenge. Before the General Court in Boston he charged Kezia Coffin with aiding and abetting the enemy (she had entertained some of the raiders and, he claimed, had pointed out his warehouse as a likely target). He also leveled treason charges against Dr. Benjamin Tupper, one of the island's most outspoken Tories, and the three Nantucketers who had tried to negotiate with the raiders: William Rotch, Timothy Folger and Samuel Starbuck. Evidently Jenkins' complaint against them was that they had not prevented the raiders from making off with much of his belongings.

The unlikely combination of defendants sailed to Boston. Phineas Fanning accompanied Kezia and John Coffin to handle their defense. The defense was successful, and daughter Kezia Fanning wrote in her diary that her parents "came home in W. Rotch's vessel . . . Mama is in perfect health."

Mama's problems, however, had just begun. Her monopoly was disintegrating. Other Nantucketers were finding ways to slip through the blockades, which became spottier as the war's end neared. Then, with the war over, Nantucket's vengeful neighbors ganged up on their hated Tory.

Customers boycotted Kezia Coffin's store. Debtors refused to pay. Nantucket's court took a sympathetic view of those who had assumed mortgages during the war, and refused to foreclose on many of them. When there was a foreclosure and a house was put up for auction, the Nantucketers banded together and refused to bid it up; one ludicrously low bid would be made, no one would top it, and Kezia would lose another part of her assets.

She was short of cash and in debt herself. Expecting to collect on the mortgages she held, she had bought up land around the island, accumulating her own mortgages. Now she found herself in a crunch. On one side, her debtors refused to pay; on the other, her creditors were taking her to court. Phineas Fanning was a busy man.

He could not stem the tide. Finally one lawsuit resulted in the loss of the house and store on Centre Street. When the sheriff's deputies came to carry out their orders—with undisguised pleasure, according to young Kezia—John Coffin walked out of the house. But Kezia Coffin refused. Her daughter wrote in her diary that the deputies "took up her chair and carried her out of the house and set her in the street." Kezia Fanning also commented: "I am fearful my beloved parents will lie in the street, and I believe it is the wish of many."

Kezia Coffin was not beaten yet. To her lawyer son-in-law she said, "I want thee to keep this in court as long as I live." She discovered another avenue to investigate. An Act of Parliament was passed in London to reimburse American Loyalists who had suffered losses because of their allegiance to the king. A commission was established in Halifax for this purpose, with May 1, 1786, the deadline for claims.

When Kezia heard of this opportunity it was almost too late. She left Nantucket on April 18, the very day her house had been seized and she had been carried out into the street. Her ship encountered bad weather, and she did not reach Halifax until May 18.

She stayed on, repeating her claim and trying to collect. The commission refused her. She ran up heavy debts. Her creditors took her to court, and she was sent to debtor's prison. For six weeks, hungry and ill, she was confined to a cell with no furniture except a mattress on the damp floor. When she was released in July 1787, she discovered that she was a widow.

Destitute and disillusioned, John Coffin died in Nantucket the same month that his wife finished her term in the debtor's prison in Halifax. Kezia returned to Nantucket more determined than ever. Once again she went back to Halifax to press her claim for reimbursement. Once again her claim was rejected. She returned to Nantucket and launched yet another campaign in the island's court to recover what had been taken from her. Phineas Fanning was pressed into service again on what looked like a never-ending series of court appearances.

It happened that he was not with her on March 27, 1798, when she had another frustrating day before the judge; Phineas and Kezia Fanning were in Boston on a visit. Kezia Coffin returned home alone, went up the stairs toward her bedroom and, on the top step, suddenly fell backwards. It may have been a heart attack, it may have been a stroke. She was sixty-six years old.

Her daughter and son-in-law returned that evening. Late that night Kezia Fanning wrote in her diary that her mother "was taken up for dead, but about 9 o'clock she revived so as to speak several words, but did not know her own sister—she soon fell in a snoring sleep, and such was her situation when I first beheld her surrounded by her brethren and my dear children."

The tough old lady lingered for two more days and died on March 29. Her son-in-law, who had dutifully kept Kezia's lawsuits in the courts, now quietly let them lapse. He died, at only forty-eight, nine months later. His last child was born in March 1799, three months after his

death. The younger Kezia remained on Nantucket. She
started a school, which did not succeed. She continued
to record Nantucket's doings in her inimitable diary. Her
children all moved off-island. And when Kezia Fanning
died, on November 20, 1820, at sixty-one, her children
inherited her diary. An abstract was made of it by her
grandson, Thomas Fanning Wood, at the behest of Alexander Starbuck for his *History of Nantucket.* But the complete fifty-volume diary has never been found.

Her mother's life provided material for at least two
works of fiction. The first, in 1834, was by Col. Joseph
C. Hart: *Miriam Coffin or The Whale-Fisherman.* In this
novel Kezia becomes Miriam and John becomes Jethro.
The author draws the moral that woman's place is in the
kitchen, not the store. Herman Melville found Hart's
book useful in helping him describe Nantucket in *Moby
Dick,* which was published in 1851, a year before Melville
visited the island. A much later novel was *Nantucket
Woman* by Diana Gaines, who presents a Kezia Coffin
with a sexual appetite to match her strong will and even
includes an attempted seduction by Cousin Ben Franklin; it was the talk of Nantucket in the summer of 1976,
not all of the talk favorable.

The house on Centre Street was burned to the ground.
The country estate at Quaise was rebuilt so many times
that it is unrecognizable. Nor is there anywhere around
the area a sign of the tunnel in which Kezia Coffin is
supposed to have secreted her ill-gotten goods.

Her stubborn spirit lived on, though, in the years that
followed, as Nantucket's men went to sea for longer and
longer voyages and Nantucket's women were thrown
more and more on their own devices. In effect, they ran
the island. They were father as well as mother to their

children. The pressures on them were great, greater than most of their husbands realized, for the men were preoccupied with their own arduous lives. In his observations on Nantucket, Hector St. John de Crèvecouer claimed that most Nantucket women were habitual users of opium, to help them through their dreary, husbandless days. No other evidence has been found to support this claim; Crèvecouer evidently heard it from Dr. Benjamin Tupper, a notorious Tory and a somewhat malicious gossip.

Certainly the Nantucket women's nights were lonelier than their days, and one predictable result was a higher than normal proportion of divorces. Owen Chase, first mate of the ill-fated *Essex,* survived his open-boat odyssey after his ship had been sunk by a whale to return and divorce his wife for adultery. He had four wives during the course of his lengthy career away from Nantucket. Robert Cathcart, master of the *Otter,* was at sea when he received word that his wife had been unfaithful; he sailed into the nearest port, sold the ship and kept the proceeds —perhaps an understandable method of repaying the *Otter*'s owner since it was he with whom Mrs. Cathcart had sinned.

Not all the whalemen remained innocent when they found themselves far from home in the Pacific, surrounded by willing island women. The biggest brothel area in Honolulu was called Cape Horn because of the saying that the American whalemen hung their consciences on the Horn on the way out and picked them up again on the way home.

But most of the whalemen and their wives somehow managed to adapt to their unnatural lives. One departing captain is reputed to have responded to a friend who reminded him that he had not said goodbye to his wife: "Oh well, never mind, I shan't be gone more than a year or so." One wife, says a Nantucket legend, greeted her husband on his return from a four-year voyage with: "Hello, Si. Here, get a bucket of water. Dinner is almost ready." And a new minister on the island, unaccustomed to the tradition of asking for the congregation's blessings for departing whalemen, and betrayed by a misplaced comma, read to his flock a message thrust into his hand: "Captain Peter Coffin, having gone to see his wife, desires the prayers of the congregation."

Some of Nantucket's hardiest women were those captains' wives who decided that they had had enough of their lonely existence on the island and decided that life on a whaleship, with all its hardships, was preferable. It was crowded in the captain's cabin. They had to manage their children's schooling themselves. And it was a brutalizing life for the women and children. Still, these women and their children had their own ameliorating effect on many whaleships. Far from disliking the presence of a captain's family, many whalemen enjoyed the sight of children on board, and even more appreciated the improvement in the food and the luxury of having a seamstress aboard. One crew in particular could thank the wife of Captain John Norton of the whaleship *Ionia*. Some of them had tried to jump ship at one of the tempting tropical islands, but they had been caught in the act and were tied to the rigging when the aptly named Charity Norton came on deck.

"John," she asked, "what are these men in the rigging for?"

"I'm going to lick 'em," the captain explained.

"Oh no, you're not," said Charity. And that was the end of that.

Nantucket's best-known whaling wife was Mrs. Charles Grant. Her husband was scarcely back from a voyage in 1849 when there was a knock on the door. Mrs. Grant said, "Charles, if that is Mr. Macy after you to go whaling, you ship me too." Mrs. Grant shipped out on her husband's whaling voyages for the next thirty-two years. One son was born on Pitcairn Island; a daughter was born at Bay of Islands; another son was born on Opolu Island. No doubt inspired, and certainly comforted, by the presence of his family, Captain Grant brought home more whale oil than any other Nantucket captain.

Life on a whaleship was nevertheless as difficult a test of Nantucket's hardy women as anything they survived at home. It was movingly described by Mary Hayden Russell, who in 1842 wrote from aboard the *Emily* to her daughter half a world away, reporting a typical day on a whaling voyage and pondering, in frugal Nantucket fashion, the lesson it taught her.

The *Emily*'s boats had lowered for whales on a threatening afternoon. By dusk only one boat had returned, with a whale. Its bulk dragged at the ship as they tried to find the other two boats. Through a violent thunderstorm they kept up their search and at last, after four hours, found them. "Think, my dear Mary Ann," Mrs. Russell wrote, "how anxious I must have been, and how happy I was to see your dear Father once more. . . . He had not a dry thread in his clothes. I thought this is the way these sons of the ocean earn their money—that is so thoughtlessly spent at home."

Quaker Burial Ground,

ONE of the social centers of Nantucket is the barnlike structure on South Water Street called the Dreamland Theater. Every time we go there I am reminded of a Japanese friend who was taken for the first time to the New York Philharmonic. Afterwards his host asked him which selection he liked most. "The first," he replied. "Yes," his host said, "Beethoven's Third Symphony is

9
THE QUAKERS

Upper Main Street

internationally popular." "No," said my Japanese friend, who much preferred Japanese music, "I meant the one before that, when the musicians were tuning their instruments."

Often the best show at the Dreamland is the period before the lights go down and the movie starts. For this is the time to enjoy the infinite variety of Nantucket's summer population, ranging from weather-beaten old characters in long-billed caps to fresh young things in the latest mod shirts and clog shoes. The old characters, of course, are summer visitors, and the young mods are islanders.

It is also a time when you can survey the structure of this vast hall and guess how much of it still remains from the original building, designed as a house of worship. In the 1830s there was a schism among Nantucket's Quakers; a splinter group constructed their own meetinghouse on Main Street. When the meetinghouse was sold, it became a hat factory. Later it served as a dance hall (no doubt to the horror of the surviving Quakers). In 1883 it was moved out to Brant Point to become part of the structure that was called Hotel Nantucket. The hotel failed, and in 1905 the building was moved again, to its present location, where it was first a social club and now entertains Nantucketers both before and during the movies.

It would be difficult, no doubt impossible, to tell what part of the present Dreamland Theater was what part of the Quaker meetinghouse, or even to figure out how much of the original has survived the many moves. But the contrast between the lively scene in the movie house and the somber proceedings of last century's Nantucket

Quakers does tell us a lot about how the island and the islanders have changed.

Early Nantucket and Quakerism were inextricably entwined. But not all of the assumptions are correct. Let us return to that first settlement and see how it did begin.

It did not begin with Quakers. Nantucket was not, as is often claimed, founded by Quakers. As we saw in the case of Thomas and Sarah Macy, Nantucket's first settlers were refugees from the Massachusetts Puritans. Thomas Macy was in trouble with the Puritans because he had sheltered some Quakers for an hour and a half one rainy morning, but he was not a Quaker himself. Nor were the other original purchasers of Nantucket Quakers. Like Macy, they were repelled by the abuses of the mainland Puritans, and they simply wanted to put as much distance as they could between themselves and the bigots of Salisbury.

As a result, the first Nantucket settlement was unique. Unlike nearly every other community in New England, it had no religious overtones. There was no church. In fact, for the first half century after the settlers' arrival the only religious observances on the island were those of the Indians.

The missionary work of Thomas Mayhew and Peter Folger had resulted in regular church services among the Indians. They seemed to have no difficulty adopting the religion of the missionaries, which was largely Presbyterian, and adding some aspects from their own. One white observer says that the Indians' religious meetings were serious, sober affairs, following the catechism of the church. "And when the meeting was done," he added, "they would take their tinder box and strike fire and light their pipes, and, maybe, would draw three or four whifs and swallow the smoke, and then blow it out of their noses, and so hand their pipe to their next neighbor. And one pipe of tobacco would serve ten or a dozen of them. And they would say, 'tawpoot' which is 'I thank you.' It seemed to be done in a way of kindness to each other."

Meanwhile the white settlers on the island virtually ignored religion. No doubt they were reacting against the religious excesses they had escaped on the mainland. And they were preoccupied with the full-time labors of establishing their new home. Not until the beginning of the 18th century were there stirrings of serious religious belief on Nantucket, when the first Quaker missionaries visited the island. They launched a faith that would dominate Nantucket's history and shape the character of the islanders for nearly two centuries.

The first recorded visit was by a Quaker missionary named Thomas Chalkley, who sailed over "in about ten hours," he wrote in his journal, in the course of a trip through southern Massachusetts. He stayed on the island several days and induced some of the islanders to hold meetings at which the visiting Quaker could explain his faith. It was not an unknown creed to the islanders, and their interest in Quakerism was indicated by a turnout of nearly 200 at one meeting. In the course of his visit, Chalkley reported, "a friend was convinced whose name was Starbuck. . . ." It was Mary Starbuck. She was fifty-three at the time of Chalkley's first visit and had long been known as Nantucket's Great Lady. She was an important recruit.

Six years later Chalkley came to the island again. In that time Quakerism had taken hold. There were, Chalk-

ley wrote, "large meetings, people there being mostly
Friends." There was some opposition: "divers of the
people, call'd presbyterians," Chalkley recounted, point-
edly refusing to dignify Presbyterians with a capital letter, were "very cruel in their expressions, and bitter in
their spirits, against us, yet there were some who went
under that name, who were more open and charitable
towards us, and received us gladly with tenderness."

It was during the visit in 1701 of another missionary,
John Richardson, that Mary Starbuck made her first contribution to Quakerism on Nantucket: she offered her
home, the large and popular gathering place the islanders called Parliament House, for a meeting.

Richardson and a companion missionary, James Bates,
hired the sloop and services of one Peleg Slocum in
Rhode Island and sailed for Nantucket. Arriving after
dark, they went ashore and found themselves on a small
uninhabited island, probably Muskeget. Unable to get
back to the sloop in the darkness and fog, they spent the
night on the little island, sleepless and worrying that the
tide might rise over them. They found Nantucket next
day.

Richardson had already been told about Mary Starbuck, and he asked directions to her house. "At the first
sight of her," he wrote in his journal, "it sprang to my
heart. To this woman is the everlasting love of God."

Mary Starbuck at once consented to a meeting in the
Starbuck house next day. Richardson described that
meeting with details that illustrate the fervor of early
Quaker meetings, considerably unlike the sober meetings held in later years.

The Starbuck front room, so large that the islanders

referred to it as the Great Hall, was cleaned and polished for the occasion. Benches and chairs were lined up, with the visitors facing the already-acknowledged Friends. The windows had been removed and more seats were provided in the yard outside the front room. The only thing Richardson missed was a platform to stand upon, "for I was not free to set my Feet upon the fine cane chair, lest I should break it."

It was a large assemblage, sitting in Quaker silence waiting for the Lord to move one of them to speak. When one did—Richardson's fellow missionary, Bates—he was surprised to be answered by a heckler. It was the local Presbyterian minister, who thereupon left the meeting.

Richardson next felt moved to speak, which he did at length. As he spoke he kept his eyes on Mary Starbuck. He saw her "sometimes looking up in my face with a pale, and then with a more ruddy complexion; but the Strength of the Truth increased," Richardson wrote, "and the Lord's mighty Power began to shake the People within and without Doors." As for Mary, Richardson reported, "When she could no longer contain, she submitted to the Power of Truth, and the Doctrines thereof, and lifted up her voice and wept."

The session thereupon took on the semblance of a revival meeting. The rest of the assembled people were caught up in the semihysteria. "Oh! then the Universal Cry and Brokenness of Heart and Tears was wonderful!" Richardson rejoiced. "From this time I do not remember one word I spoke in Testimony. . . ." In fact, Richardson recalled that he began to feel faint. He "made a motion to break up the meeting, but could not do so for some time, for they sat weeping universally." He warned those nearest him that he might faint; still the weeping went on. "But after some time," Richardson wrote, "Mary Starbuck stood up and held out her Hand. . . . I observed that she, and as many as could well be seen, were wet with Tears from their Faces to the fore-skirts of their Garments, and the Floor was as though there had been a shower of rain upon it." Mary Starbuck came to Richardson and asked, "What shall I do for you?" Richardson replied that he could use a drink—"not strong, but rather warm." As he followed her out of the room, he wrote, "I felt Sweat in my Shoes as I walked."

Peleg Slocum, whose sloop had brought the Quakers to the island, said after this meeting, according to Richardson, "that the like he was never at." Indeed, it must have been an impressive occasion, even assuming some pardonable hyperbole in Richardson's account. Certainly it confirmed Mary Starbuck not only as a Quaker but as a leading Quaker on the island. Shortly she and her husband and most of her children and their spouses officially joined the church. Many of the Quaker meetings were thereupon held in the Starbucks' Great Hall, and everyone was awed by Mary Starbuck's eloquence whenever the Lord moved her to speak.

So fast did Quakerism grow that only five years later it was suggested that the members build their own meetinghouse. There followed two or three years of procrastination, no doubt because of the expense. There seems to be no record of when the first meeting house was built, or where, although historian Henry B. Worth believes the land was donated by the Starbucks, so it must have been near their home alongside Hummock Pond.

In 1713 the Nantucket Friends voted to donate thirty

shillings to aid in the construction of a meetinghouse in Dover, on the mainland; the Nantucketers would hardly have felt able to make such a contribution if they were still building their own. Only three years later the Friends voted to enlarge their present meetinghouse. Quakerism was expanding at an impressive rate on Nantucket.

Evidently it had its share of zealots. Quakerism involves a belief in direct communication with God; it is not anticlerical so much as nonclerical, with every Quaker his own minister. The Quakers who came to Nantucket and the islanders who joined the faith believed in an Inner Light that came to them as true believers and showed them the way of God. In its outward manifestations Quakerism appeared sober, serious and drab. One of its fundamental tenets was a denial of all worldly pleasures, which were regarded as frivolous; dancing, drinking, card-playing, even music belonged to the "World's People," who were scorned as wastrels and sinners. Ornamentation, often any sort of beautification, was also scorned.

Beneath this drab surface ran a strong current of pious zeal that often bordered on fanaticism, particularly in these earlier days. In fact, the Puritans who persecuted the Quakers in the Massachusetts Bay Colony had some reason. Far from being submissive martyrs, Quakers in Massachusetts would gather and hoot at the governor when he walked down the street. They would interrupt the services of other churches with shouts or heckling. One Quaker stormed into a church, held up two bottles, smashed them together and shouted: "Thus will the Lord break you all in pieces." Perhaps the most eye-catching protest, at least to the Puritans, was made by two Quaker girls named Lydia Wardwell and Deborah Wilson, who claimed they were "testifying before the Lord" by running naked through the streets.

Not quite the Quaker image we have accepted over the years. But what these Quaker excesses indicated is an understandable point about nearly all religions: they are not so absolute as they claim to be. Religions of almost any sort tend to adapt to regional circumstances. Compare a service in New York's St. Patrick's Cathedral with one in an Italian hill town church, or the Zen meditations in Kyoto and in San Francisco, and you will get the idea. So while some of the persecuted Quakers in the Massachusetts Bay Colony ran amok, a very different type of Quaker evolved on the island of Nantucket.

The difference, of course, was that these were Nantucket Quakers and the key word was Nantucket. They may have gone into hysterics at that first meeting with John Richardson in Mary Starbuck's house. But as Quakerism influenced more Nantucketers in succeeding years, the Nantucketers influenced Quakerism even more, molding it into their own form of religion.

Thus it became pragmatic and flexible, useful to the Nantucketer because many of its tenets were what the Nantucketer needed, but not dominating him or very much changing him. To the hard-working, frugal islander, Quakerism had many attractions beyond the religious fervor expressed in John Richardson's one-sided account.

Quakerism was inexpensive. It required no salary for a minister and no parish house for his family, because every Quaker was his own minister. Moreover, a Quaker

family had no incentive to—and in fact had a strong
religious incentive not to—waste money on such frills as
fancy clothes or any ornamentation. Spinets, music
boxes, games, parasols and other expensive luxuries
were proscribed. Simplicity and plain living was not only
preferable, it was also less expensive.

Yet the pragmatic Nantucketers knew how to adapt
even Quakerism to their lives. Plain living did not mean
poor living. A Quaker dress might not have buttons (the
invention of the devil), but the cloth and cut could be the
finest. A Quaker home should have no unnecessary ornamentation, but its design could be ample and comfortable; some of Nantucket's handsomest houses have the
simple, utilitarian lines dictated by Quakerism. And
while it was a sin to flaunt wealth, it was no sin to make
money. Of course, a good Quaker should not use illegal
or immoral methods. But Nantucketers were good at
sailing close to the wind.

One Nantucket Friend, a shipowner named Jacob
Barker, set an example. Barker became concerned about
one of his ships; it was overdue and was not insured. He
called at the office of an insurance company and asked
to take out a policy. The premium represented a nice
profit for the insurance company—unless, of course, the
ship were lost. The company's investigators tried to find
out the whereabouts of the ship, meanwhile preparing
the policy. Shortly Friend Barker reappeared, announcing that he had heard from his ship and adding, "If thee
hasn't made out that policy, thee needn't." The insurance company representatives quickly responded that
the policy had indeed been made out and was ready.
Barker sighed and said he'd pay the premium; he had

asked for the policy and refusing it now would not be a
Christian thing to do. Signing the policy and paying the
premium, he remarked: "Yes, I've heard from her. She
went to the bottom off Hatteras last month, with all on
board."

The Nantucket Quaker was equal to an even greater
test of his faith during the American Revolution. When
he could stand by his faith unequivocably, he did, often
with ingenious solutions to the dilemma. William Rotch,
whom we have described as the conscience of Nantucket
during the American Revolution, found himself in a
quandary over some bayonets in his possession. Before
the war he settled an account with the estate of a deceased debtor by taking in trade a number of muskets,
some equipped with bayonets. Nothing could be more
anathema to a Quaker than a bayonet. A musket could
be used for hunting, which was not proscribed by the
Quakers. But a bayonet could only be used against another human being, and that was one of the worst sins
for a pacifist Quaker.

So William Rotch did a good business in muskets,
mostly to whale fishermen who wanted them for bird
shooting while in the northern waters. "Whenever those
with the bayonets were chosen," he wrote later, "I took
that instrument from them." The muskets were all sold,
and the bayonets gathered dust in his warehouse.

War came, the Continental Army scoured the countryside for arms and someone remembered a bayonet he
had not been able to buy from William Rotch. The
Quaker merchant was asked for his bayonets; they were
badly needed by the Army. Rotch replied: "As the instrument is purposely made and used for the destruction of

mankind, I can put no weapon into a man's hand to destroy another." He was asked again. He repeated his refusal. "It made a great noise in the country," he recorded, "and my life was threatened." So Quaker Rotch found a practical solution: "I took an early opportunity of throwing them into the sea."

Other Nantucket Quakers had other practical methods for sticking to pacifism. It was because of their Quaker beliefs—supported by the realization of their exposed position—that led the Nantucketers to petition both the American and British governments for recognition of the island's neutrality during the Revolution and the War of 1812. Some Quakers found patriotism more compelling than religion, and they broke with their church to go to war. Others found ways to maintain their neutrality. When Loyalist Refugees were terrorizing Nantucket, a decidedly non-Quaker islander named Benjamin Bunker, just returned from privateering, decided to sail out and teach them a lesson. A choice vessel for such an expedition was the fast little craft belonging to Captain Nathaniel Paddock. Bunker asked Paddock to contribute his boat to the cause. Paddock politely explained that as a Quaker he could not be part of any such "use of violence." But in an aside he mentioned that the keys to the cabin door were wrapped in the mainsail. Bunker "stole" the vessel and used it in what he also called a "Quaker victory," since he captured a Refugee vessel with scarcely a shot being fired.

Another Quaker captain, whose name has been lost, found himself closer to the action during the War of 1812: he was becalmed in Vineyard Sound and was being overtaken by a rowboat from a British privateer. His first mate proposed readying a swivel gun on the stern. The Quaker captain refused. The mate proposed that the captain go below while the mate assumed command of their defense. The captain consented. As the boat approached and the mate took aim, the old Quaker poked his head up the companionway and said, "Mate, if thee means to do any execution with that swivel, I'd advise thee to lower the muzzle a little."

Another Quaker captain responded to an attack by Malay pirates in the East Indies by waiting until the first one started climbing a rope on the ship's side, then cut loose the rope, saying: "Thee can have the rope, Friend, but thee can't come aboard." And when confronted with an obdurate skipper who was hogging space at a wharf in New York, a Nantucket Quaker captain called to his notoriously profane mate: "Friend Peter, come up here and use some of thy unadvised language on this man."

The Nantucket Quaker was, in short, adaptable. When the Second Congregational Society was having difficulty raising enough money to install the famous Portuguese bell in its tower, one Quaker, Obed Mitchell, made a contribution, explaining his seeming defection from his Quaker faith by saying: "Friends do not use bells for religious purposes. But as they are very useful in giving fire alarms, etc., I will assist in the purchase."

The women were adaptable, too, if only in learning how to set a Quaker bonnet at a slightly rakish angle and to flip a Quaker shawl so as to enhance a provocative profile.

Quakerism profoundly affected Nantucket and Nantucketers. During the height of its popularity it gave the islanders, at the very least, an excuse for choosing hard work and frugality over indulgence. At best Quakerism provided the incentive that made Nantucket the world's center of its chosen industry, whaling. Nantucket Quakers were among the first to preach against slavery, and to practice what they preached. While Elihu Coleman was one of America's first abolitionists, William Rotch put his principle into practice at a time when there were still slaves on Nantucket. One slave owner, John Swain, tried to reclaim a black who had shipped out on Rotch's vessel, the *Friendship.* When the *Friendship* returned, Swain claimed his slave, named Prince Boston, and the man's share of the voyage. Rotch refused to hand over the slave or his money. Swain sued, lost in the Nantucket court and appealed to Boston. Rotch engaged a promising young Boston attorney named John Adams. The suit was dropped. Swain tried to repossess his slave by force. Rotch and the *Friendship*'s captain, Elisha Folger, hid the slave and helped him escape to the mainland. Soon, and partly because of this example, all slaves on Nantucket were freed.

Nantucket Quakers were not only among the earliest abolitionists and American pacifists, they also campaigned for women's rights long before it was a popular issue. Such Nantucket women as Lucretia Mott and Anna Gardner are still remembered as leaders in the women's suffrage movement.

Quakerism also left a legacy of functional beauty in the narrow streets of Nantucket town. The Quaker houses are attractive because they are unostentatious. Their durable craftsmanship still appeals to the eye and to the viewer's sense of proportion. And the plain, utilitarian, comfortable interiors of these houses remind us, especially in our times, of the virtues of the simple life.

Moreover, the times were right for Quakerism on Nantucket. Perhaps a religion nearly always flourishes best in adversity. During the 17th century, when Nantucketers were struggling for their existence, the Quakers' ranks grew. The meetinghouse that had been built in 1713, and had to be enlarged in 1716, was too small for the swelling numbers of members by 1730. A 17th-century Quaker version of a fund drive was launched, and in 1733 the director of the drive reported on his collections: £11.14s8d. from the men and three times as much, £34, from the women members. The new meetinghouse, on the corner of Saratoga and Main Streets, was a much larger building than the old, and was not completed until 1736. It served the purpose until 1793, when once again more room was needed.

The American Revolution did not diminish their numbers. Some Nantucket Quakers went to war, and were expelled by their pacifist brethren. But as many more became new members. By that time nearly all the Nantucketers had moved from the Capaum Pond area to the present town, and the location of the meetinghouse on Saratoga and Main Streets had become inconveniently far from most members' homes. So it was voted to move this meetinghouse into town, where it was reinstalled at the northwest corner of Pleasant and Main Streets. At the same time another was built a few blocks away, at the corner of Broad and Centre Streets. The older building was designated South Meeting House and the new one North Meeting House. An off-islander visited both meetings in 1794 and reported that there were 113 families in North Meeting and 220 in South. The Quaker elders divided the island into two sections, and the members in each section attended their respective meetinghouse.

This period was the high-water mark for Nantucket Quakerism, and it lasted for roughly twenty more years. Nantucket was struggling to recover from the Revolutionary War. The town was growing, and the population was earnest, hard-working and single-minded. The plain living and industrious precepts of the Quakers were suited to these Nantucketers.

Yet, perhaps inevitably, Nantucket's Quaker influence began to fade. Its denial of most of the worldly pleasures of life could not stand up through succeeding generations in the unimaginable prosperity that came during the mid-19th century. Stern, square houses gave way to ornate mansions. Nantucket's architecture became almost a revolt against Quaker tradition. The revolution continued with the pianos and portraits, whist tables and whiskey decanters of the golden age of whaling.

But more important was a change in the attitude of the Quaker elders. They seemed to forget the flexibility of their forebears. The early Quakers had known how to trim their religious sails to the wind. The Quakers of the mid- and late-19th century met criticism and disaffection head-on. And their major weapon could only be self-defeating: they read the dissidents out of the meeting—excommunicated them—thus reducing the number of Nantucket Quakers at the very time that their faith was becoming less popular.

Schisms developed. The Quakerism that had survived the Coffin-Gardner feud in earlier times was damaged by the mutual recriminations at the time of the Bank Robbery and by the internecine disputes of the Sheep War. The War of 1812 divided the island as had the Revolutionary War, this time with a greater effect on Quaker membership. After the war a great many islanders moved to the mainland, little realizing that Nantucket's greatest prosperity was to come. Again the depletion in the Quakers' ranks was not filled.

By 1829 the drain was so great that the two meetings had to be consolidated. North Meeting was dissolved, and the remaining members transferred to the meeting-house on Pleasant Street. Watching their membership shrink, the Friends squabbled among themselves. Petty tyrannies were imposed by the elders. Not only ornamental clothing but all buttons and buckles were frowned on; one woman was put "under dealings"—threatened with excommunication—because she wore gold-rimmed spectacles; the umbrella was proscribed. Not even the dead were spared: the Friends regarded gravestones as ostentatious. And when one widow, fearful of not being able to find her husband's grave, planted a wild rose over it, the Quaker elders excommunicated her.

Meanwhile more and more of the liberal Friends were rebelling against the denial of art, poetry and music. Music, one Quaker elder proclaimed, "produces hysteria and weakens females for motherhood." Maria Mitchell, the astronomer, evidently considered this pronouncement unscientific. As a young girl she helped her sister buy a piano and hide it at a neighbor's house. One day while their parents were out the Mitchell girls had the piano moved into their own home. The parents returned to be greeted by piano music. Mrs. Mitchell was horrified. Mr. Mitchell laughed and asked: "Play something lively."

Shortly he was visited by a delegation of Friends who

warned him that the Mitchells had been put under dealings because of the piano. Mr. Mitchell responded by
suggesting that it seemed unwise for the Quakers to
threaten to excommunicate the cashier of the bank that
held the mortgage on their church. The piano stayed.
Maria never learned to play it, but she did something
worse: she played whist. And she defied the Quakers.

Others revolted against the Friends' insistence on
such biblical names as Amaziah, Abishai, Micajah, Jedi-
diah, Zephaniah, Hepsibah, Merab, Bethiah. So the
times had changed and the climate on Nantucket was
different when a major Quaker schism developed on the
mainland. Many Nantucketers were quick to respond.

In 1828 a Long Island farmer named Elias Hicks led
a liberal group out of the orthodox Quaker ranks. The
"Hicksites" made their major break and their headquarters in Philadelphia. But Hicksites were soon appearing
on Nantucket, and by 1831 there were enough to erect
their own meetinghouse. This was the beginning of the
end for Quakerism on Nantucket.

The Hicksites were promptly disowned by Nantucket's
Quaker elders. More and more Nantucket Friends
reacted by joining the Hicksites. Within two years the
new group had outgrown its meetinghouse, abandoned
it and bought another building on Fair Street. Today you
can see both of these buildings, the Fair Street meetinghouse in its present role as part of the Nantucket Historical Association, and the original meetinghouse in its
reincarnation as the Dreamland Theater.

The two sects became known as the Hicksites and the
Orthodox Quakers. They had nothing to do with each
other. The Orthodox Quakers responded not by temper-

ing their rules but by further repression, driving more and more of their flock to the Hicksites. Other splinter groups formed, further weakening the faith.

But even the more liberal Hicksite Quakerism could not bend to Nantucket's increasingly modern ways. Nor did the end of Nantucket's golden age mean a rebirth of Quakerism. It was too late. The membership figures tell the story. In 1795, at the height of Quakerism's popularity, when Nantucket's population was less than 5,000, there were 1,700 Friends. In 1845, with the population nearly 10,000, there were 300 Friends. By 1900 Nantucket's population was down to 3,000; the Quaker population was down to 0.

Just before the turn of the century, on a stormy Sunday (or First Day, as the Quakers called it), the last two Quakers on Nantucket, a man and a woman, met for the Monthly Meeting in the Fair Street Meetinghouse. The man was an elder, so he sat on the elders' bench on the men's side, at the head of the meetinghouse. The woman sat on one of the lower benches on the women's side.

In the silence, as each waited for the Inner Light, only the sound of the storm could be heard. Finally the elder was moved to ask the other Friend if she would like to come up and join him on the elders' bench. She declined, explaining that she was "not worthy." For an hour they sat and listened to the storm whistle around the old meetinghouse. Then the elder rose, came down the aisle and walked up to the woman. They exchanged a sober handshake. With that the last Monthly Meeting of Friends on Nantucket ended, and the two old Quakers walked out into the storm to go their separate ways.

IN the course of visiting Rotch's warehouse, the Dreamland Theater and the Whaling Museum, and in walking
up Broad Street and down Centre Street to the Pacific
Bank, we have also nearly circumnavigated the business
center of Nantucket. At least the area bounded by Main,
Centre and Broad Streets and the wharves on the waterfront comprised virtually the entire business district in

10
"ONE-THIRD OF OUR TOWN IS IN ASHES"

the 19th century. You can stand on the steps of the
Pacific Bank and see nothing but shops, stores and office
buildings to your left and straight ahead. Now imagine
a clear view from here to the harbor, broken only by
blackened chimneys rising out of a carpet of smoking
ashes.

That is what you would have seen on the morning of
July 14, 1846. For all of the previous night, since 11 P.M.
on the 13th, indeed an unlucky day for Nantucket, the
heart of the town had been one roaring inferno. The
catastrophe is still known as The Great Fire, a milestone
event in Nantucket's history.

Yet it seems more surprising that Nantucket had not
been consumed by fire before 1846. Especially during
the whaling period, the town was a tinderbox ready to be
ignited. With its rows of wooden houses huddled together, dried by the salt air for a century and heated by
huge screenless fireplaces; its wharves and warehouses
jammed with barrels of oil; its narrow streets funneling
the strong winds—Nantucket must have been a fireman's
nightmare.

The town's first pumper was purchased as early as
1750. Fire cisterns, like underground hydrants, were laid
beneath the streets starting in 1803. But Nantucket did
not have a fire department as such until 1838, when
twenty volunteers were provided with some hoses, buckets and a pumper and officially designated as a fire-
fighting unit. Not that there had been no fires before this.
A frequent site was the lighthouse on Brant Point, with
its oil lamp and its location open to the wind. The lighthouse burned to the ground in 1759. It was rebuilt, then
burned again in 1782; it was rebuilt the same year, only

to burn down again the next year. But evidently its isolated location kept the fires from spreading into town.
Great Point Light, erected at the eastern end of the island in 1784, stood for thirty-one years before it burned
down, whereupon it too was rebuilt only to burn down
the following year.

To some extent it was because of Nantucket's vulnera-
bility that isolated fires like these were kept under control. Nantucketers, for all their lack of a full-fledged fire
department for so many years, were fire-conscious.
Nearly every house had its buckets for sand and water,
and many interior doors had "fire panels" with glass
panes through which an incipient fire could quickly be
seen. The rooftop walk served a purpose besides that of
a lookout: from the walk a bucket of sand or water could
quickly be dumped on a chimney fire. The town's church
towers were manned with fire watchmen as early as 1787.

Still, there were a few close calls. Brant Point seemed
particularly flammable; in addition to the recurrent lighthouse fires, several houses on the point burned in 1769.
The oil-soaked wharves frequently erupted; one fire on
South Wharf in 1812 started in a blockmaker's shop and
burned nine buildings on and near the wharf before it
could be extinguished. Yet in the early 1830s Obed
Macy, in his *History of Nantucket,* could point out with
some pride that in an entire century the total loss to fire
on Nantucket had been less than $37,000.

Such complacency disappeared in 1836. Just before
midnight on May 11 of that year, a fire started in the rear
of the Washington House, a hotel on Main Street; a wall
evidently ignited from the heat of the kitchen chimney.
Before the fire could be curbed it spread to the next-

door home and store of Francis Hussey, and to William
Swain's hardware store on the corner of Union Street.
Cowan's tailor shop next to the hardware store was in
flames before the firemen finally managed to confine the
conflagration. That one fire caused more damage than
all those Obed Macy had listed in the one hundred years
before it. Then, on June 2, 1838, came another big one.

It should have been excellent, if frightening, training
for The Great Fire to come in 1846. It started unnoticed
during the night. At 2 A.M. flames spread through Joseph
James's ropewalk in the rear of Union Street. The tarred
hemp caught quickly, and the flames were fed by oil and
pitch until the ropewalk erupted in a ball of fire.

Fanned by the wind, the fire and burning debris flew
toward the waterfront and wharves. Some casks of oil
were stored in the ropewalk; burning oil flowed down the
drains and out into the marshes near the waterfront,
spreading a sheet of flames under the wharves. The oil-
soaked planking caught immediately, igniting hundreds
of oil casks in the warehouses and sending a sheet of
liquid fire across the harbor. The buildings on the
wharves roared and exploded during the night.

Firemen trying to quench the flames found that a ditch
along Union Street had filled with burning oil from the
ropewalk and was blocking them with a curtain of fire.
They quickly decided to contain the conflagration instead of fighting it. Four homes, a store and a workshop
were blown up with gunpowder to form an open lane and
halt the spread of the fire.

Still it raged for four hours, lighting up the night and
consuming nearly thirty buildings. Dozens of homes
were leveled, as well as the oil warehouses, cooper's

shops, sail lofts, paint stores, a twine factory, a boat-builder and several other buildings. An attempt to save a load of lumber by floating it on a raft failed when the burning oil on the harbor surface spread around the raft and swallowed it up. Next day all that remained in the swath between Union Street and the harbor were brick chimneys and walls, blackened hardware and the iron hoops of oil casks, lying in rows where the wooden staves had burned away from them. In the still-steaming harbor were the charred ends of pilings where the wharves had burned to the water's edge. So fierce had been the heat that there was scarcely any charcoal left, and so strong the wind that the wreckage was nearly free of ashes.

Nevertheless, everyone agreed that the firemen had done an excellent job of confining the disaster area. And the *Nantucket Inquirer* predicted in an editorial that "no fire in Nantucket can ever be so extensive and alarming."

Six years later there was a fire that was not so extensive but nonetheless tragic: on February 21, 1844, the Poor Farm at Quaise burned to the ground. Five men and five women, some of them bedridden, died in the fire. Forty-nine others, and the keeper and his family, escaped into the cold winter weather. It was the largest death toll by fire in Nantucket's history.

Then, in 1846, came a little blaze in a hat shop that, almost incredibly, exploded into Nantucket's Great Fire. This is how it happened.

It had not rained for several days preceding July 13, 1846. The atmosphere had been drier than usual, with few of Nantucket's famous fogs bathing the wooden buildings. At 11 P.M. a fire smoldered and burst into flames in the hat shop of William H. Geary, in the block between Orange and Union Streets on Main Street. There was a fire watchman on duty in the Tower of the Unitarian Church, but he could see nothing; the flames were still confined inside the hat shop. But a passerby in the square did see smoke coming from a window in the shop, and the alarm was sounded.

Nantucket's fire department was subdivided into brigades, or companies. There were sixteen cisterns set in the streets of the town—flagstones with iron rings covering outlets connected to the underground water system. Two of the fire companies responded. Both had big hand pumps on wheels: the one pulled by Fire Brigade Number 6 was called "Cataract"; the other, belonging to brigade Number 8, was the "Fountain." They came rumbling across Main Street's cobblestones, both arriving at the hat shop at the same time. There was a cistern in Main Street near the hat shop. Both fire companies raced for it, and the trouble began.

By Nantucket tradition, the first company to arrive at the scene of a fire had the honor of hooking up to the nearest cistern and pumping the first stream of water on the flames. Both companies claimed that honor. There were arguments, an altercation, and the two hand pumps stood idly in the street while members of the fire companies argued over precedence. While they were wrangling, and before a hose could be connected, there was a crackling boom and the fire roared through the roof of the shop.

A small group of people had already gathered, and one of them later contended that the flames inside the hat shop could quickly have been doused if one of the pumps had been connected during the critical minutes while the two fire companies disputed each other's priority. Now, in a fiery burst, burning debris flew onto the roofs of adjoining buildings.

Several seemed to ignite at once. The breeze was light, but the fire evidently needed little fanning. While the call went out for more fire companies, the growing crowd of bystanders watched the flames spread up and down the south side of Main Street.

The selectmen and the fire chief quickly tried to organize things. There was now plenty of work for both fire companies, and all the others were called out. The remaining cisterns on Main Street were tapped and water poured onto the flames. But within the first hour so many buildings were ablaze that streams of water from the pumpers were pitifully useless. The fire marshals convened to try to work out strategy.

The flames appeared headed up Main Street toward the old part of town. Once the fire was loose among all the houses packed together back of the business district, the whole town could go up. Again the fire fighters decided to try the forest fire technique of clearing a lane to halt the spread of the conflagration. They selected some houses at the head of the square and prepared to sacrifice them. Kegs of gunpowder were rushed to two houses on the corner of Orange Street. Their owners objected but were hurried out as the kegs were trundled into their houses and ignited. In a chain reaction, both houses exploded.

But the fire had created its own violent updraft. Flaming chunks of wood soared into the night sky and arched across the square like a fireworks display.

At the head of the square stood the solid brick struc-

ture of the Pacific Bank. On the south corner was Philip
Folger's brick house. The firemen tapped into the cistern
in front of the bank and played their hoses on the roofs
and wooden trim to protect these buildings. On the roof
of the Pacific Bank was a wooden cupola housing the
little observatory of its cashier, William Mitchell; here,
through Mitchell's telescope, his daughter Maria had discovered her famous comet. The cupola burst into flames.
The firemen, working frantically at their pump handles,
managed to get up enough pressure so the water from
their hoses reached the roof. Although the cupola continued to burn, the hose-soaked roof of the bank did not
catch.

The gunpowder seemed not to have halted the spreading flames. Instead, it sent more burning debris into the
air and onto other roofs. By midnight nearly all of the
square's south side had become one gigantic blaze.
Clearly the fire was out of control.

The only hope seemed to be more fire lanes to confine
the fire if it could not be controlled. Fire wardens raced
up Main Street beyond the Pacific Bank. The first large
house in this section was the home of John Barrett, president of the bank. John Barrett was at the bank, watching
William Mitchell's cupola burn and praying that the rest
of the roof would not catch fire. At his home a fire warden was met by Mrs. Barrett. He directed her to clear
everyone out because they would have to blow up the
house to curb the onrushing flames. Lydia Barrett
refused to leave: if they blew up her house, she announced, they would have to blow her up with it. Cursing
with frustration, but with no time to argue further, the
fire warden retreated. By the time he got back to the

square, he could see that the fire had crossed to the north side.

The light breeze blowing earlier in the evening had now become a strong wind—the fire's own wind, created by its roaring updraft. And the wind had shifted from east to south. Mrs. Barrett's house was saved. But the entire business section of the town was now in the path of the fire.

Down Main Street it raced, touching off one building after another on the north side. From both sides of the square the fire advanced on William Rotch's counting-house, now an insurance office, at the head of Straight Wharf. The building's roof erupted. Flames licked at the wooden windowsills. The heat smashed the glass. The brick walls stood, containing a flaming pyre that consumed the interior and leaped into the sky.

Other flames rushed down Centre Street, igniting a line of wooden shops like a string of firecrackers. As more firebrands filled the air, the buildings east of Centre Street, toward the waterfront, were embroiled in the conflagration. Driven by its own wind, and beyond the control of men with water pumps, the fire headed for the oil-soaked wharves and the vast stores of explosive whale oil in the warehouses at the waterfront.

By this time all of Nantucket was in the streets, some helping the firemen and many more getting in the way. A few wealthy islanders managed to bribe some workers to wet down or remove goods from their own houses and stores. Others pleaded with and shouted at fire wardens who were trying to blow up their homes. One couple stood in the door of their home helplessly watching the fire approach. A burning piece of wood soared across the

sky and landed on their roof. They did not see it land,
but within minutes they were running for their lives as
flames spread through the house.

The entire business section of the town—office buildings and stores, the Town Hall and Post Office, banks
and churches—were surrounded by the advancing
mountains of fire. It had become a huge holocaust of
deafening noise: the booming, crackling roar of the
flames was punctuated by the crash of walls, the smashing of glass windows and the occasional explosion of
more gunpowder. It was as bright as noon, and the light
in the sky that night could be seen far at sea. Nothing
could now be done except stand in this dancing hell and
let the fire consume itself.

Firemen watched the flames engulf the Atheneum Library; there was not even time to remove the priceless
collection of whaling exhibits that had been on view on
the building's second floor, and all of them were destroyed. On Centre Street only the Methodist Church,
set back on the west side, escaped immolation, its pillars
blackened as the fire raced past. At the corner of Centre
and Broad Streets and sheet of flame leaped across to
ignite the new Trinity Church and houses alongside it.
The Jared Coffin house, the building resembling the
Three Bricks on Main Street, escaped; its brick walls
slowed the fire and turned it eastward, helping save the
rest of the town to the north and west. The fire ran down
Broad Street to the wharf, at about the same time that the
flames to the south reached the waterfront. And then
came the climactic pyrotechnics.

The wooden wharves and cooper's shops and ropewalks and boat sheds and lumber yards all seemed to

flame up at once. Fed by the years' accumulation of pitch and oil and grease, they roared and smoked and crackled as even the town's wooden buildings had not. Then the hundreds of oil casks stored in the warehouses exploded in booming bursts like an uneven cannonade. Sheets of liquid fire poured onto the streets along the shore, and as the burning oil spread across the water, the harbor itself became a sea of fire. Small boats and even larger vessels were swallowed up in the seething cascade.

The fire consumed itself in that final inferno. By dawn there was little left except smoldering embers and clouds of smoke. William Macy later wrote that he stood on the steps of the Pacific Bank and looked out at the vessels beyond the bar, outside the harbor. There was nothing to block his view except the stark, black chimneys rising out of the ashes like gaunt trees in a desert.

Providentially, not one person was killed. But thirty-six acres and at least fifteen blocks were gone. It was the heart of Nantucket, the shops that had provisioned the town and the businesses that had provided a living for the townspeople—not to mention the homes among these shops.

Nantucket's selectmen met amidst the ashes to consider relief for the destitute. One of their first moves was to send an eloquent appeal for aid to nearby cities and towns on the mainland.

One-third of our Town is in ashes. A fire broke out on Monday evening last, a few minutes before eleven o'clock, and raged almost uncontrolled for about nine hours. The whole business section of the town is consumed. There is scarcely a dry goods, a grocery or provision store left standing, and what more particularly threatens immediate distress, the stocks contained in them, so rapidly did the conflagration extend, are almost utterly destroyed. There is not food enough in town to keep wide-spread suffering from hunger at bay a single week. Seven-eighths of our mechanics are without shops, stock or tools—they have lost really even the means of earning bread. Hundreds of families are without a roof to cover them, a bed to lie upon, and very many of them without a change of raiment. Widows and old men have been stripped of their all; they have no hopes for the future, except such as are founded upon the humanity of others.

We are in deep trouble. We cannot of ourselves relieve the whole distress, and we are compelled to call upon those who have not been visited like ourselves, for aid, in this our hour of extreme necessity. We do not ask you to make up our loss, to replace the property which the conflagration has destroyed, but to aid us, so far as you feel called upon by duty and humanity, in keeping direct physical suffering from among us, until we can look round and see what is to be done. We need help—liberal and immediate. If we seem to you importunate, we can only say that could you look upon the yet smoking ruins of one-third of our Town—could you walk through our remaining streets filled with houseless hundreds wandering about seeking for some roof to cover them, or for such remnants of their household goods as may have been snatched by others from the flames— could you feel, as we do, that not many days pass before positive want will be knocking at our doors—our words would appear feeble, our appeal certainly not more earnest than the occasion requires. But we are confident that you will feel for us and with us and that you will render us such assistance as is in your power....

Please direct anything which you may send to the Selectmen of the Town of Nantucket, and we pledge ourselves to dispense whatever you may bestow, faithfully and, to the best of our ability, judiciously.

Nantucket's neighbors responded with $100,000— about one-tenth of Nantucket's loss, but a welcome contribution to immediate relief. Within two months most of the disaster area was being rebuilt.

It has often been said that The Great Fire brought an end to the golden age of Nantucket. Its timing was unfortunate, because whaling was already in decline. But there were other contributions to the decline. The California Gold Rush seduced nearly four hundred Nantucketers, some of whom jumped ship on the West Coast; others shipped out from the island, a few even taking along their houses, knocked down into sections. Only a few returned, most of them poorer than when they had left. Then came the Civil War, in which most of Nantucket's remaining fleet was driven from the seas. There was a death watch atmosphere on the island. But the coup de grace, as we have seen, was the refinement of kerosene, which replaced the whale oil on which Nantucket depended for its livelihood.

Coup de grace indeed. For, in a sense, it could be argued that the decline and fall of the Nantucket of the 19th century was a blessing in disguise. At the time the blessing, in Winston Churchill's phrase, seemed to be exceedingly well disguised. But Nantucket's vicissitudes —the decline in whaling, The Great Fire, the desertion of Nantucketers to the gold fields—forced Nantucket into the 20th century. That, however, is another chapter.

*Auld Lang Syne (1675)
—older than the 'oldest house'?*

LET us leave Nantucket town and head east to Siasconset. Go down Orange Street, once the street of the whaling captains, then the street of inns and now noted chiefly for Mitchell's Book Corner at the square and, near the other end, the Nantucket Bake Shop, home of Portuguese bread. Keep going past the shops and Our Island Home to the traffic circle and the offices of an-

11
REVIVAL

'Sconset Pump (1776)

other Nantucket institution, the *Inquirer and Mirror.* Turn east.

Do not try this trip by bicycle, unless you ride for many miles as a regular thing. Nantucket's gently rolling hills are deceptive. Take your car, rent one, or join one of the guided tours; from your window you will see dozens of panting, exhausted bicycle riders pumping home and obviously wishing they had been less ambitious.

By car you can take the long route, bearing left to get an occasional view of the big harbor and the quiet little settlement of Wauwinet. Or you can head straight down the main road to your goal, Siasconset, the village that saved Nantucket. In the center of this pleasant hamlet you can stop by the 'Sconset Pump (which is the same age as the U.S.A.), look around you and understand how it all happened.

There was something about Siasconset even from the beginning. The Indians preferred this end of the island. And the settlers had hardly established themselves on the big harbor before some of them were migrating farther eastward to this cliffside at the leading edge of the island.

The cliff stands 100 feet above the sea and is Nantucket's highest point. In its layers of glacial debris and "Sankaty Sand" you can read its geological history. And from the edge of the cliff you can survey the sea for a dozen miles to the east and south.

That is what led the early Nantucketers to this jumping-off spot of the island. The first whaling lookouts were raised here and along the south shore. Fishermen also came here bringing their dories to launch for codfish in the spring and fall and bluefish in the summer. Soon they realized that the miles of rutted roads across the moors amounted to an impossible daily commute, especially since the best fishing time was early in the morning. The answer, of course, was to throw up crude lean-to's in which to spend the night.

The fishing was good. The fishermen spent more and more time in their shacks, and improved their comforts. Understandably, their wives began to wonder what was going on out there at the other end of the island, and went to see. They were captivated by the lonely beauty of the place. Inevitably the lean-to's became more substantial cottages for the whole family, and as early as the mid-17th century, the cluster of fishermen's shacks became a summer resort for many Nantucket families.

Let me recommend another intriguing book. It is *Early Nantucket and Its Whale Houses* by Henry Chandlee Foreman, a professional architect who has done a fascinating bit of detective work in Siasconset. Studying the configuration of the oldest houses, Foreman has come up with persuasive evidence about which structures are the oldest, what has been added to them since, and how they still reveal the evidence of those early days when the fishermen came out to the eastern end of the island to camp during the weeks when the cods and the blues were running.

On the basis of his detective work Foreman claims that two of Siasconset's houses are older than Nantucket's so-called "Oldest House." The typical fishing shack of the 17th century, he points out, was a snug one-room affair with a ladder to the sleeping loft. Cooking was done in an open lean-to back of the shack. But when the wives arrived and decided to turn it into a vacation home, another room or two were added. "Warts" they were called, because of the way they grew like protuberances on the main body of the original fishing shacks. Distinguishing the shacks from their warts, Foreman concluded that the central portions of two Siasconset houses were the oldest remaining structures on Nantucket Island.

One is called "Shanunga." Foreman estimates that its central portion was built as early as 1681; the ells were added later when some fisherman's family decided to move in. The name Shanunga is a great deal newer than the house; it comes from a ship wrecked on Siasconset's shore in the 19th century. The house also served as a tavern; the taproom measured 8 feet by 10 feet (and rum was 3 cents a glass). Later it was the Siasconset Post Office when it belonged to Captain William Baxter, who daily brought the mail from the boat in Nantucket town.

The oldest house on the island, Foreman maintains, is the one aptly named Auld Lang Syne. Again the central part is the original fisherman's shack; it may have been built as early as 1675. Both houses still show evidence of the old sleeping loft and the tiny room in which the fishermen spent the few hours when they were not out in their boats. Thus if Foreman is right—and there are historians who dispute him—these ancient houses, sturdily built of driftwood from shipwrecks plentifully provided by Nantucket's shoals, predate the official "Oldest House," the Jethro Coffin house in Nantucket town, by as much as eleven years.

So Siasconset was a summer resort as early as the 17th century. To an extent it was even earlier, when the Indians brought along their hides and stretched them over stakes in the ground to spend the summer months fishing and chasing whales. The name Siasconset (pronounced "Sconset") probably comes from the Indian word "Missiaskonsatt," meaning "near the great whalebone." But it was Nantucketers of the 18th century who turned Siasconset into what one mainland observer called "the Newport of the Nantucketoise." And it was Siasconset that in the 19th century rescued Nantucket from becoming a ghost island.

Not that the Nantucketers had given up. There was a mass emigration from the island when whaling went into decline; by 1875 the total population was down to 3,201. Those who remained tried to find ways to provide employment and sustenance for the Nantucketers. In fact, in the 1830s, while whaleships were still going out, some Nantucketers tried to start a silk factory. Reasoning that the island's comparatively mild climate would sustain mulberry trees on which silkworms would flourish, they planted hundreds of the trees. In 1836 they constructed a silk mill, importing looms, spinners and bobbins from the mainland. Shortly the Atlantic Silk Company was producing vests and handkerchiefs that were praised by all, even winning a silver award at a fair in New York State. But Nantucket turned out not to be a good area for mulberry trees, or for silkworms. The proprietors of the Atlantic Silk Company got into a dispute. Within eight years the mill closed down and the mulberry trees were left to wither away with the Nantucketers' hopes for another industry.

There were a few attempts at other businesses. Some small factories were geared up to manufacture various products, but the extra expense of shipping raw materi-

als to the island and returning finished products to the
mainland made the ventures uneconomical. A shoe factory was started in 1859; it failed. Another was started in
1872 and succeeded for a while; but it too closed after
a few years. In 1880 John Hallett made 50,000 linen
dusters; but it was not long before he went out of business like all the others.

Nineteenth-century Nantucketers turned from whales
to a less ambitious fishery, and for a while Nantucket was
a highly productive source for the New York and New
England fish markets. Again, the greater cost of doing
business 30 miles from the customers was too much.
Nantucket even today has a healthy fishing business, and
Nantucket scallops are particularly prized. But it is far
from a large enough industry to support the entire island. Instead, what did save Nantucket from declining to
a sleepy fishing village were the off-islanders. And as
much as the first white off-islanders altered the Indians'
Nantucket, the latest off-islanders have transformed
Nantucket and continue to do so.

What started this transformation was the little village
on the eastern bluff. In the early 18th century it was still
a fishing station—dirty, smelly and infested with fleas.
The fishermen's wives started a clean-up, and by the turn
of the 19th century Siasconset was becoming an attractive hamlet of cottages looking out on the wide beach
and the open sea. By mid-century the word had spread,
not only to Nantucket town but to the mainland. Nantucket's well-known historian, Obed Macy, wrote, "As a
summer resort no place in the United States presents
greater attractions." Indeed the town and its setting
were "admirably adapted to refresh and invigorate both

mind and body." Tourism to the island started with a
trickle rather than a rush. And had it not been for Siasconset, the vacationers might not have discovered Nantucket for another century. As early as 1842, while whale
ships were still sailing for the Pacific, and in fact two
years before the erection of Sankaty Head Lighthouse,
there was an Atlantic Hotel in Siasconset, and the village
on the bluff had become the favorite summer home of
hundreds of mainlanders.

The major attraction was a sense of being at sea, far
from the turmoil of the cities. Few ocean vistas could
match the view from Sankaty Head, with nothing but
ocean between the beach and Europe 3,000 miles away.
Thoreau came and was impressed. His friend Ralph
Waldo Emerson also visited Siasconset, stood on the
bluff and marveled at the gusts blowing the tops off the
waves, "like the hair of a woman in the wind." The sense
of quiet peace in the village of tiny cottages was another
attraction. And as more visitors came to enjoy it, thereby
threatening it, one 'Sconseter was quoted as saying, "We
are not willing to barter away the moral character of our
little village in exchange for the dollars of our summer
visitors." To an extent they did, of course. And therein
lies the paradox of today's Siasconset and Nantucket: the
very qualities that attract the visitor are endangered by
the visitor.

Siasconset, however, provided for Nantucket's rejuve-
nation by introducing the new industry to replace whaling. And it was already nurturing this industry before the
old one was gone. There is a fallacy in the assumption
that the island of Nantucket went into a deep sleep in the
middle of the 19th century and did not wake until the

20th. Tourists were coming to Nantucket in the 1840s. The island's salvation, if that is the word, had already started decades before kerosene replaced whale oil and spermaceti candles. What happened was that tourism was a much smaller business than whaling in those years. And the most substantial part of the business—the summer-long resident—was in Siasconset.

So while Nantucket town became impoverished, Siasconset grew at a rapid rate. A typical case was that of a carpenter in Nantucket town who was unemployed so long that he quit the business and built himself a tiny place at Siasconset, intending to spend the rest of his days fishing and growing his own vegetables. Within a few months he was asked by an off-islander to build a summer home; by the time he was finished, he had another order. He went back into the carpentry business, at Siasconset instead of Nantucket town.

The lack of building, of development, of "growth" in Nantucket town had its peculiar advantage. The attractive flavor of the town is largely provided by the 18th- and 19th-century character that was preserved with so little change during the turn of the century when Nantucketers could not afford the bad taste that the mainlanders could. Rare is the Victorian monstrosity in Nantucket town. Meanwhile, what saved Siasconset was the very simplicity of its cottages: those crude fishing shacks so attracted the newcomers that they emulated them in their own houses.

Slowly tourism did revive the entire island. By 1842 the steamer *Massachusetts* was making a daily run between New Bedford and Nantucket. The voyage took ten hours and the fare was $2, without meals. In 1846 the steam-

ship company bought, for $7,000, the brick home of
Jared Coffin, the one that had turned the fire of 1846,
and converted it into the Ocean House to accommodate
the growing tide of tourists. And by 1874 there were two
boats a day during the summer. But Siasconset was still
a major attraction, despite the arduous ride over the
rutted roads to the end of the island. The south shore
began to attract some of the newcomers, and in 1881 a
railroad was laid across the island to Surfside; the link to
Siasconset was completed three years later.

Still, the revival was a gradual process. In 1882 part of
Surfside was carved into building lots; but despite the
new railroad, no town sprang up. A similar project on
Coatue, complete with bathing pavilion and a small
amusement park, also failed. To some extent, while the
island may not have been gaining in quantity it was gaining in quality. During the ebb in the town's fortunes,
many of the old houses began to deteriorate, and grass
grew between the cobblestones on Main Street. But now
the island began to attract visitors of sufficient substance
to save and restore the old houses and even the Main
Street mansions. (They could be bought for less than
$500, but their restoration was expensive.) One off-islan-
der built his own mansion on the "Cliff," as the highest
part of Nantucket town is known. He was Charles O'-
Conor, a wealthy New York lawyer, and he imported
marble from Italy for his fireplaces, reminding Nantucketers of the days of Joseph Starbuck and his Three
Bricks. O'Conor was generous as well: in 1884, just before his death, he personally paid off the town's entire
debt of $7,000.

It was not undiluted quality, of course. Nantucket

could, and still can, attract an unattractive breed of vacationer. A favorite island anecdote concerns a youngster
attempting to profit from tourism by peddling pond lilies
to the summer visitors. At the Ocean House he encountered an off-islander who was not interested in lilies but
asked, "What do you sell when there ain't no pond lilies?"

The boy replied, "Oh, sometimes one thing and sometimes another."

"Humph! Don't you go to school?"

"Yes, sir."

"Oh, they have a school here, then, do they?"

"Oh, yes, sir."

"Well, what do they learn you in school?"

"Why, they teach us grammar and other things."

We have seen that an island's isolation, sometimes
combined with inbreeding, can encourage eccentricity.
And no doubt an influx of visitors can add its own en-
couragement. Nantucket, and particularly Siasconset,
offered a rich variety for the tourists' entertainment. The
most prominent of the town's eccentrics was "Billy"
Clark, a self-professed town crier, who went about the
streets blowing a horn, announcing the news, occasionally with comment, and broadcasting advertisements,
with little of the distinction expected today between the
news and the commercials—in fact, frequently without
pause for breath. A typical Clark performance would be:
" 'Nother severe murder in New York! Man killed his
wife, then killed himself—both of them dead! Meat auction on the lower square tomorrow morning at 10 A.M."
Billy Clark often seemed to be everywhere at once, and
was known to climb the Unitarian Church tower for bet-

ter results. To many of his townspeople he was a nuisance; but visitors found him quaint and amusing, especially if they were subjected to him for only a week or two.

Siasconset's contribution was William Baxter, "Captain" of a craft named *Swiftsure,* a wagon in which he made the run at least once daily between Siasconset and Nantucket town. He advertised that the *Swiftsure,* which he coyly referred to as a "sidewheel craft," was for charter "newly rigged, and is supplied with hard cushions for invalids and soft seats for sweethearts. Deaf ear turned to cooing and billing." But his chief function was to carry the mail from the town to Siasconset.

Baxter set up his own Post Office in his home, called Auld Lang Syne, the oldest house on the island. Every day the *Swiftsure* went across the sandy road to town; Baxter picked up all the mail for Siasconset and set out for home; as he came over the last rise before reaching the town he sounded a trumpet, the signal for all 'Sconseters to gather at Baxter's Post Office. By the time the *Swiftsure* churned around the corner, the rail fence in front of the house was occupied by a row of youngsters perched like birds, waiting for the mail. The fee was one cent per letter, to pay Baxter for his special delivery. Later in the afternoon the 'Sconseters would hear another blast from Captain Baxter's trumpet. The *Swiftsure* was bound out for Nantucket town, and anyone with outgoing mail had better get it down to Baxter's Post Office in a hurry.

It was a typically informal—and in fact illegal—Siasconset arrangement. Captain Baxter pocketed the extra penny he charged to bring Nantucket mail to Siasconset.

His daughter Love Baxter served as unofficial postmistress, collecting all outgoing mail. And it led to the sort of confrontation with officialdom in which islanders delight. Someone reported to Washington that a man named Baxter had a sign over his house reading POST OFFICE, whereas in fact Captain Baxter was not an employee of the United States Post Office. The letter went from office to office in Washington; appropriate stamps and signatures were affixed; copies were made; and an investigator was sent to the island to inquire into the transgression.

Like nearly anyone else debarking from the steamboat in Nantucket and asking for transportation to Siasconset, the Post Office inspector found himself aboard the *Swiftsure*. Captain Baxter inquired of his mission. The inspector seized the opportunity to ask if Captain Baxter had seen an unauthorized Post Office sign in Siasconset. Baxter said: "I live right there in the village, and I'd be sure to know it if there was such a sign there, but I never saw it. However, the best way will be for you to see for yourself." Whereupon he drove the postal inspector to Polpis, some 10 miles north of Siasconset, and took the inspector past every house in town. No Post Office sign. Captain Baxter drove the inspector back to town. The inspector got on the next boat, returned to his office and reported that there was no substance to the accusation. And Captain Baxter's Post Office in Siasconset continued to do business. A few years later it was in fact officially recognized by the U.S. Post Office; Love Baxter became Siasconset's postmistress, at a salary of $12 per year.

Siasconset not only had its own characters, but it at-

tracted a good many from the mainland. At the turn of
the 20th century the village became the summer resort
of dozens of actors and actresses from New York. Their
names may not be immediately recognizable to the present generation, but at one point about half of the Lambs
Club, the New York gathering place for actors, was sum-
mering in Siasconset. The main street of town was renamed Broadway. DeWolfe Howe entertained his neighbors with his classic recital of "Casey at the Bat." George
Fawcett, his wife Percy Haswell, Regan Highston, Frank
Craven, Isabel Irving, Frank Gillmore and his daughters
Margalo and Ruth, plus dozens of other actors and actresses known to all theatergoers of the time, formed a
colony at Siasconset—until air-conditioning made it possible for the real Broadway to stay open in July and
August, and Siasconset's actors' colony could no longer
take the summer off. (A delightful memoir of these days
is Margaret Fawcett Barnes's 'Sconset Heyday.)

While Siasconset and the rest of the island enjoyed
their new prosperity, they began to recognize a paradox.
The whaling industry did not contain the seeds of its own
destruction. So long as there was a demand for whale oil
and Nantucket whalemen could supply it, the islanders
were prosperous. It is quite possible that if whale oil
were still in demand, Nantucket would still be one of the
capitals of the world. The sandbar in front of the harbor
would have been surmounted had it been necessary for
the island's survival. In fact, of course, it has. When the
old industry was made redundant by kerosene, the new
industry—tourism—also required a safe passage into the
harbor. So the long-proposed jetties were built; they
were completed in 1889, at a cost of just under half a

million dollars. A new channel was dredged, and the
jetties kept it from filling up again. No bar formed across
the jetties' mouth, despite the predictions.

Only in recent years has it become apparent that Nantucket's new industry may be self-destructive. Columnist
Russell Baker, a frequent Nantucket visitor, has put the
problem succinctly: "The dilemma of the American vacation, of course, is that what is good for vacation business
is bad for the vacationer."

Nantucket's problem, in fact, is almost the world's
problem in microcosm, as it confronts the explosion in
population. For more than a century, while the tourist
industry slowly expanded and then began to accelerate,
Nantucket seemed big enough to absorb the growth.
The influx became island-wide. Siasconset still attracted
many devotees, but its growth slowed. The cross-island
railroad failed to make a profit, partly because storms
kept undermining the tracks along the south shore.
When World War I provided an opportunity to sell the
rails and rolling stock to the government to ship to
France for troop movements, the railroad was torn up.

An immediate result was the introduction of the automobile. And here was one of the first examples of the
inevitability of mechanical progress. For some years
Nantucket's town fathers had tried to ban the automobile
from the island. In a 1914 referendum the town had
asked the Massachusetts Legislature to pass a special act
excluding autos from the island, and the Legislature had
obliged. Then, in 1918, after a strenuous campaign by
auto advocates and a few test cases, the islanders re-
lented and voted to repeal the act; within a week there
were eleven automobiles on the island; within three

months there were ninety-four. And everyone knows what the Main Street square is like today on a busy morning in August; no doubt many modern Nantucketers walk as far from the nearest parking place as the early Nantucketers who did not have cars.

Despite the influx of automobiles, Nantucket's rolling countryside remained largely undefiled. The influx was seasonal. And in recent years much of it has been daily, as the "trippers" come over from the mainland for only a few hours of sightseeing and shopping. But by the 1970s the population pressures began to be felt. Where there is demand there will always be people ready to supply it at a price. And as land and house prices rose, the "developers" became a significant and highly controversial element in Nantucket's future. The developer, by carving up a piece of land into small lots and throwing up houses or condominium apartments, could make a little bit of Nantucket available to off-islanders who never thought they could afford it.

The developer is a natural result of a prosperous tourist industry. The visitor who is so attracted to an area that he returns every year understandably starts thinking of purchasing his own piece of the place. And if someone offers him a small vacation home—even an apartment in a high-rise building—he becomes at once a potential Nantucket resident, and a potential threat to Nantucket.

He himself realizes the latter (although he would never put it that way) only after he has become a resident. A dramatic change comes over him. Suddenly he is concerned about the proliferation of the very sort of habitation he has just bought. He realizes that among the attractions of Nantucket are the open countryside, the

barren moors, the uncrowded beaches. And now that he
has his piece of Nantucket he becomes concerned over
the possible loss of these attractions. One Nantucketer
describes this attitude as "We've got ours; now stop the
island."

Nantucketers have reacted to this threat in different
ways, and to an extent the reaction depends on whether
he is an islander or an off-islander. The latter has generally reacted by 1) trying to limit further crowding of the
island and 2) trying to protect the character of the island.
An organization called The Nantucket Conservation
Foundation, for one, has purchased large sections of
Nantucket with the intention of preserving it and protecting it from exploitation. Nantucket's selectmen and
voters, encouraged by off-islanders, have protected the
island from many abominations of the mainland: there
are no neon signs, no parking meters or pay toilets.
There is not even a traffic light, although one or two
might be helpful. The town has also instituted what may
be among the world's most stringent zoning laws. A
home owner anywhere on the island, for example, may
not alter or even paint his house without abiding by
Nantucket's guidelines or getting permission for any de-
viation from these rules.

That, in essence, is where most off-islanders and islanders disagree. The off-islanders accept, or claim to accept, an article of faith that is erroneous: that overcrowd-
ing and altering the character of Nantucket would be
economically harmful. It is, alas, a false assumption.

There are sections of Fire Island, off the south shore
of Long Island, New York, to which the defenders of
Nantucket can point with horror: eyesores they are, but

economically they are quite healthy. There are crowded sections of Martha's Vineyard that make one nostalgic for the fishing villages they have replaced; that nostalgia is not shared by the fishermen's children who sold the house and land for a price so high they could scarcely believe it. For a generation our family took a short vacation every winter in Nassau, then a pleasant, inexpensive Bahamas island with empty beaches and uncrowded inns. On what was certainly our last visit some years ago, Nassau had become another Miami Beach and even our best-hidden coves were defaced by high-rise hotels. Nassau had been destroyed for us, but certainly not for the Bahamas government, which makes two or three times as much from mass tourism as it ever did, or will, from the likes of us.

In short, Nantucket may, and probably will, eventually lose its traditional charm; but in the process it will not lose money. Hotels may sprout at Nantucket Airport. Condominiums may march up Monomoy. High-rises may soar above Siasconset's bluff. A pity, but no economic loss. Imagine the price of an apartment looking down on Sankaty Head Light. Call it, if you like, a contradiction of capitalism.

It is this confusion of values that underlies the biggest battle on Nantucket since the Coffin-Gardner feud, and one that affects the island's future more than whether it "secedes" from Massachusetts to join another state. The conflict was stirred up by a law proposed to the U.S. Senate by Senator Edward Kennedy. Called the Nantucket Sound Islands Trust Bill, it attempts to protect these islands in somewhat the way the National Seashore reservation on Cape Cod does for that area, by establish-

ing a reserve protected by law. In a somewhat oversim-
plified description, the Nantucket Sound Islands Trust
Bill would carve up Nantucket Island into three areas: 1)
a "forever wild" section that in effect would become a
national park; anyone already living in this area would
have to move out five years after the area became a park;
2) a "scenic preservation" area in which present building
could remain but no further building could be done; and
3) a "town" area, which could be developed as the islanders wished.

The islanders reacted adversely to Senator Kennedy's
bill for a number of reasons. The senator is not popular
with everyone on the island. Nor is Kennedy's chief
proponent of the bill on Nantucket, a man named K. Dun
Gifford, whose family has been visiting Nantucket since
1880, but who was described by an islander with the
ultimate put-down: "Dunnie's a yachtie; he lives up on
the Cliff." There was also the natural tendency to resent
regulation from the mainland, especially from Washington. One islander expressed this philosophy succinctly:
"No bastard is going to tell me I can't keep lobster pots
on my front lawn." But the major reason for the Nantucketers' objection to the Islands Trust Bill was economic—whether they would openly admit it or not.

Nantucket's economy once depended on whaling. The
smell of burning whale oil was unpleasant, but it was
worth it. Today's tourists do not smell as bad as yester-
day's tryworks—at least not yet—and a Nantucketer can
put up with a lot of damage to his island if it means his
livelihood. He will regret it; he shares the off-islander's
appreciation of the natural beauties of the island. But
like the off-islander, who perhaps made his money de-

spoiling some other area, the Nantucketer likes to feed and clothe his family. And he has long ago learned the lesson of tourism, which is that quantity is usually more lucrative than quality.

The Nantucketers went on record, 392 to 12, opposing Senator Kennedy's bill, even though in the course of discussion and investigation it was discovered that developers have already made plans for doubling the present number of houses on the island. Whatever the fate of the bill, it will not be popular among the year-round residents of Nantucket.

And of course it is more than an economic argument. There is a strong ecological motive for protecting the island's fragile heaths and not polluting the surrounding waters. There are some who cite a responsibility to the island's first inhabitants, even before the Indians: the fauna. The island's history has been a succession of off-islanders turning the island and the islanders to their own purposes: the Indians hunting the fauna, the white settlers changing the island's economy so that the Indians died out, and the present off-islanders changing the island's economy again.

The islander vs. off-islander theory is tempting and deceptive. Few of today's off-islanders spend more than a month or two on Nantucket, so one might say their influence is proportionately even greater. Moreover, there are different types of off-islanders, and they affect the island in different ways. The "day trippers" who come over on the excursion boats have little effect on the outlying countryside (except for a growing litter problem); but to a great extent they dictate the number and character of the shops in town. If you don't think so, try proposing a cutback on excursion boats and listen to the outcry from the merchants.

Then there is the "alleged" off-islander, accused by Nantucketers of coming to the island to rob the summer visitors. Nantucket's crime rate has skyrocketed as fast as that of most mainland cities. No summer resident dares leave anything of value in his closed-up home during the winter. But are these hoodlums all visitors, or are some of them island delinquents tempted by the conspicuous display of the summer people?

It is the summer resident off-islanders who have over the years made even greater changes on the island, to its benefit in the eyes of those who admire Nantucket for its open moors and uncrowded beaches. Certainly the Nantucket Conservation Foundation has protected large areas of the island simply by buying it up. The towns too have had this same sort of benefit. Walter Beinecke's restoration of a large waterfront area is more attractive than the noisome, derelict wharves he replaced. Yet his project stirred a storm of criticism. Some Nantucketers wore buttons proclaiming "No Man Is an Island," superimposed on the background of an S & H Green Stamp, the source of the Beinecke money. And instead of the restored boathouses that grace Old North Wharf, Straight Wharf is row on row of art galleries.

The art galleries are significant. They indicate yet another type of off-islander. Nantucket once attracted mainlanders who wanted to get away from it all. Nantucket now attracts thousands of off-islanders who bring it with them. Nantucket is chic. The New Yorker and Bostonian in fishing clothes and bill cap can still be seen, perhaps at the Wharf Rat Club. But his breed has been outnumbered by men in lemon-yellow sports jackets and women in Italian slack suits with lightship baskets on their arms.

It is the Nantucket lightship basket that virtually epitomizes today's Nantucket: it has a history, it is attractive and it is a status symbol. The history goes back to the South Shoals Lightship, which was first anchored 24 miles south of Sankaty Head Light in 1856, to mark the shoals that extend that far south of the island. The crew of ten was confined to a 103-foot ship for four-month tours of duty, with nothing to do but clean the wicks and chimneys of the two lights, keep the vessel shipshape, stand watches, eat and sleep. Like their ancestors at sea for years on the whaleships, the lightship crew members developed a hobby to ease the long hours of idleness. The modern scrimshaw became a basket. The original basket goes back even further, to the Indians who first inhabited the island; you will recall Abram Quary asking that his baskets be included in his portrait.

These sturdy containers were woven from rattan and topped by wooden handles. The farmers adopted them and adapted them, strengthening them by adding a wooden bottom, but no top. The lightship sailors copied these baskets. Only a few added a top, still unlike the basket seen everywhere on the island today.

In 1905 the South Shoals Lightship was automated and the crews came home. Some of the older men continued to make the baskets ashore. In one case the tradition went down through a family: Charles Wray made lightship baskets on the lightship and on the island, and his son Mitchell took up the art. On some of Mitchell Wray's baskets was a label reading:

I was made on Nantucket!
I'm strong and I'm stout.
Don't lose me or burn me,
And I'll never wear out.

That was the lightship basket's chief appeal: it is so
well made of such strong rattan that it only improves
with age. I recently saw one nearly a century old; it is
darker in color but as sturdy as ever. Another advantage
is simply that it is a basket; it stands upright; it holds
more than most purses; the contents are more easily
located. Yet the main reason for the lightship basket's
popularity among today's off-islanders, and some islanders, is its price: it is expensive, and thus it is a status
symbol.

It is expensive for good reason: it requires many man-
weeks to make. And it is not expensive over the years,
since it "will never wear out"—well, hardly ever wear
out. But there are other receptacles and other baskets
that would wear as well. What makes the lightship basket
a status symbol is that it can cost from $250 to a thou-
sand dollars, and everyone knows it. There are excellent
imitations of the real thing, most of them made in Hong
Kong and available for a fraction of the price—and any
owner of a Nantucket lightship basket can spot a Hong
Kong basket at one hundred paces.

Yet the Nantucket lightship basket is not even a lightship basket anymore. None has been made out on the
lightship on the Shoals for seventy-five years. Nor are the
present baskets like the ones that were made aboard the
lightship. The lightship basket seen all over Nantucket
today was designed by an off-islander who came all the
way from the Philippines.

José Formoso Reyes arrived in Nantucket in 1945, looking for a job teaching Spanish. Finding no teaching position, he turned to basketmaking. In 1948 he designed a top for one of his baskets. It seemed more practical than the open-top basket, and he showed it to a man named Charles Sayle who was doing a good business making ship models, name boards and scrimshaw, and selling them to tourists. Reyes asked if a basket with a top would be a popular tourist item. It was Sayles's wife who had the idea that has launched a thousand baskets: why not attach a carved figure of a whale to the top? The result can be seen on women's arms all over the U.S. and as far away as Europe. An American leaving a Paris subway one day spotted a lightship basket on the arm of a Parisienne. "Nantucket?" she asked. As the subway door closed the Frenchwoman shouted, "Oui! Nantucket!"

It is not a lightship basket in fact or design. No matter. In its way it stands for Nantucket today—not quite what it was, but attractive and valuable. And while a lot more money can be made by cheapening it, the Nantucket original remains worth caring for and preserving.

NANTUCKET is a walker's island. The only way to
appreciate the character of the town is by walking its
narrow streets. The delicate beauty of the heaths is best
seen close-up, and in fact the heath will last longer if you
don't go driving across the moors. You could walk on
Nantucket's beaches for two or three days, if you wanted
to, from Madaket along the south shore to Siasconset,

228

12
A WALK ALONG COATUE

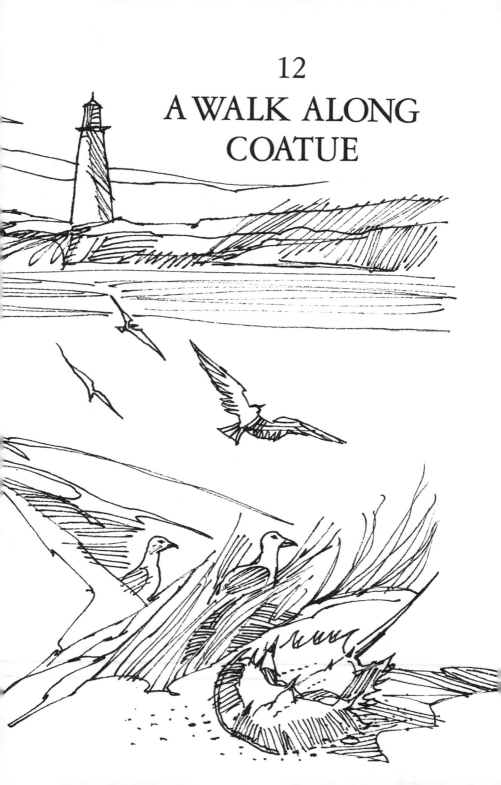

out to Great Point at the northeastern tip of the island
and back along Coatue to the town—where of course you
would be stranded, unless you are as good a swimmer as
a walker.

Not being that ambitious a walker or swimmer, I
availed myself of the boat generously provided by Cliff
and Henna O'Hara, with their house at Pocomo, across
from upper Coatue. And since the boat was powered by
the only outboard motor that has not malfunctioned as
soon as I looked at it, my wife and I set out on a sunny
September day for a walk along Coatue.

This is Nantucket's major stretch of land formed by
the sea. It is technically known as a barrier beach, a long
sandhill that was scooped up by the tide currents and
waves and deposited along Nantucket's north shore. The
barrier protects Nantucket's 6-mile-long harbor, making
most of it landlocked and providing a rich habitation for
innumerable fauna and flora in the quiet waters of the
harbor. Not being naturalists, we should have taken an
expert with us. But we took along the next best thing,
which is Dorothy Sterling's book *The Outer Lands,* to
which I am indebted for much of the identification and
lore of this barrier beach.

Coatue is a comparatively new feature of Nantucket. It
was not formed until long after the glaciers had departed
and the sea had risen to surround Nantucket's higher
hills and make them an island. This sandy peninsula is
only about 5,000 years old, less than one-third the age
of the island itself. And it is a textbook example of nature
at work constantly changing the landscape. Not only has
it provided Nantucket with an excellent harbor, it also
shelters countless varieties of fish and scallops, clams

and crabs. Above its beaches the classic dune formation has raised a low plateau adorned with plants and shrubs, alive with creatures from herring gulls to wolf spiders.

It also provides a few mysteries. How and why, for example, did the harbor side of this barrier beach form five bays of almost perfect symmetry? I was not so ashamed of my own bewilderment at this phenomenon when I found that geologist Nathaniel Shaler was nearly as baffled by it as any amateur. In his report to the U.S. Geological Survey in 1888, Professor Shaler wrote: "Coatue Bay has the most puzzling configuration of bottom and of shores of any inlet on the North American coast. . . . The configuration of the shores is even more peculiar than that of the bottom."

The geologist made a guess, however, that the "peculiar projections" that embrace these little coves "are possibly due in some way to the action of the tidal currents, which sweep up the bay with much speed and move the finely grained sand with considerable ease. From a superficial inspection it appears that the tidal waters are thrown into a series of whirlpools, which excavate the shore between these salients and accumulate the sand on the spits."

It looked like a perfectly good explanation to us as we roared across the harbor. The tide was beginning to rise, and between Pocomo Head on the island and Bass Point on Coatue the water was whirling in semicircular motion. Logic, if not geology, would suggest that just as the sands that formed Coatue built on themselves to make the barrier beach, the sands in the harbor, moving in regular patterns with the flow of the tides, would form the sandspits around which more swirling sands would

enlarge and extend these tiny promontories. (I am sure
that Professor Shaler would be gratified by my confirming observations.)

These relentless movements of water and sand have,
as Professor Shaler mentioned, also molded a peculiar
bottom to Nantucket's harbor. It is not so much one
basin as three, each relatively deep but shelving to shallows at the edge of the next one. Why?

One reason may be that the shallows are in line with
these sandspits. Nantucket harbor, then, consists of a
series of harbors, each scooped out by the tides that
whirl in circles as twice a day they travel up the lagoon
between the island and its protective barrier reef of sand.

The map of Coatue, showing these symmetrical curves
in the harborside beach, reminds us of the chambered
nautilus, the seagull's wing and so many other natural
creations that are in perfect proportion. But even this
striking example of nature at work is no more remarkable than the many other natural phenomena on Coatue.

We were struck by them as soon as we pulled the boat
up on the beach and started across the narrow strip of
sand between the harbor and the ocean. Here was a
strikingly simple example of the elementary principle by
which the primordial ooze eventually became mankind.

Dune formation. The surging seas lift a bank of sand
above the water's surface. The sun dries the sand. The
wind blows a wisp of it farther from the beach, and re-
peats the process. A tiny hillock of sand, above the tide
line, provides the foundation for a few seeds of beach
grass. One spear and then another appear above the
surface of the sand. Moisture, sucked up from the sea,
forms clouds. Rain falls and sinks into the sand, nourish-

ing the roots of the beach grass. The spears spread into clumps. More windblown sand forms around the beach grass. More grass grows. Other forms of flora take root in the spreading hillock of sandy soil. It is the beginning of a dune.

Behind the clumps of beach grass, beach peas take root, sending stringers down the side of the dune and helping to anchor it. Seaside goldenroot, a tough cousin of inland goldenrod, raises its bulky stalk; a succulent, it can store water received from rain and fog, and thus survive on its beachhead. More sand is blown up from the beach to settle around these obstacles. The dune grows in height and begins to achieve its characteristic shape, sloping downwind to the water's edge, with a drop-off on the leeward side.

In the sheltered valley behind the first dune, another forms. More beach grass springs up, followed by other hardy flora, anchoring the sandhills and building a plateau. Actually it is an undulating series of dunes, marching up from the beach. But as we walked up the slope onto Coatue's plateau it looked to us more like a gently rising hill, because the flora in the valley was so dense that it rose to the level between the protecting dunes and presented an even carpet of growth.

Just as in the primordial evolution on earth, these simple, original forms of life provided a habitation for the more complex. Behind the thin blades of beach grass rose the tough woody shrubs, bayberry and beach plum, wild rose and wild cherry—and, as my wife quickly discovered, poison ivy.

All of these flora were doing their part in converting a barren sandbank into a garden. They helped bind the

loose sand as they sank their roots to reach the water
below the surface. They flowered in season and spread
their seeds abroad to embroider the rest of the sandy
reef. Here on a barrier beach was Creation in microcosm.

Indeed, the next stage in Coatue's evolution was
everywhere around us. The fauna attracted by the flora
was busily at work propagating more flora. Bees
thrummed from flower to flower. Birds dipped in among
the shrubs to pick off seeds, which they would deposit,
fertilized by their droppings, miles down the beach. We
did not spot them, but we knew that mice and voles were
transporting more seeds through their labyrinths in the
sand.

We too are seed carriers of sorts. I can still recall our
first souvenir of Nantucket, brought back to a New York
apartment more than thirty years ago: a spray of bayberry, whose leaves withered and fell but whose white
waxy berries—the bayberry is also known as wax myrtle
—remained to remind us of Nantucket through the winter. Here on Coatue we paused to study some of the best
specimens we had ever seen, and by now we had learned
to leave it where it was. Nearby were a few bushes of
salt-spray rose, an off-island flower from the orient that
floated ashore in the 19th century from a ship that ran
aground and broke up off Cape Cod. The pink-and-white
flowers had fallen and were decaying, enriching the
sandy soil; we broke open a few of the rose hips, dodging
some mean-looking thorns, and found the rose's bony
seeds. Clearly they were quite capable of surviving the
soaking ride ashore; they now flourish amidst Nantucket's many other roses.

The beach plums and wild cherries as well had long

since lost their flowers. But their fruit was ripe. We resisted the temptation, having learned that beach plum jelly is much easier to buy than to make. And the sour wild cherries are literally for the birds.

Our plan was to cross the plateau to the outer beach, to walk along it, cross the dunes again and return along the harbor beach. The only obstacle was that flourishing menace of Coatue and much of Nantucket's countryside, poison ivy. Here on the dunes it was even more treacherous than on the moors, because in the sand it is more difficult to spot, spreading amidst the shrubs like a beach pea. Poison ivy is one of the best sand-binders in the dunes, and helps as much as any other plant to transform a barren bank into a flowering wilderness. But the poison ivy of the dunes is just as poisonous as its shrublike counterpart in the field. We had prepared for it by wearing shoes and high socks, but still we stepped warily through the dune vegetation on our way to the outer beach.

We had landed in the center of the cove between Five-fingered and Bass Points, so the distance between harbor and ocean was only a few yards. Still we saw an infinite variety of flora: woolly pincushions of beach heather, dark-leaved golden heather, carpets of reindeer and Iceland moss—tundra plants that seemed out of place on the warm September beach, as did the bright red British soldier lichens that paraded through the underbrush. And as we were about to descend to the outer beach, we spotted a particular attraction of the peninsula: the Coatue cactus. Green, spotted and prickly, it was flourishing in the sand. It is a separate species—known only on Coatue, although I could not distinguish it from the cactus I had seen across the harbor on Pocomo. Here on this sandbar was a profusion of flowers that included reindeer moss from the Arctic and cactus from the tropical desert—truly an Eden set in a salubrious sea.

And a place of contrast. As we confronted the ocean, we were struck by the difference between two beaches; in a few dozen steps we had gone from the lapping waters of the harbor to the rolling seas of the Atlantic— Nantucket Sound, actually, and with considerably lower surf than on Nantucket's south shore, but open sea compared with the quiet, confined harbor. Weed lined the beach, in layers indicating the varying tide heights of the past few days. The shore was littered with driftwood, prompting me to interrupt our walk to lug an armload of select pieces to the boat; we would have a warm and colorful blaze in the fireplace that night. I returned to be greeted by the distinctive "peep" of a corps of sanderlings. Like a well-drilled troop, they rose at my approach, flew in perfect unison out over the water and then returned in front of us, immediately resuming their flashing march along the surf line, again in exact formation. As each wave hissed up the beach, they swung expertly along its edge; then they followed its return, dipping their heads to peck at anything turned up in the backwash and to probe into the sand for grubs and mole crabs whose air holes appeared as the wave receded. Another advancing wave, another flashing run to higher ground, another pursuit of the retreating wave, all in step and so rapid that their legs were a blur.

It is hard to believe that these frail-looking little birds fly to the Arctic every year for their nesting period. But they are tough little creatures; they race along the shore like this from sunup to sunset, only occasionally stopping for a brief nap. Later on we saw a few at rest; some were hunkered down on the sand, but others were still standing. At the edge of the group was a sanderling perched on one leg, turning in the breeze like a weathervane on the beach.

Just above the tide line was the usual litter of skates' egg cases, black rectangles with tiny protuberances at all four corners. Sometimes called "mermaid's pouches" or "sailor's purses," these hollow parchments serve to protect the skate's eggs, and attach themselves to rocks or floating weed. When the eggs hatch the empty cases release their grip and float to shore, where youngsters add them to their collections of odd gifts from the sea.

Among them we found a few waved whelk cases, such tiny balls that it was difficult to believe that each one contained thousands of eggs before they hatched and the whelk cases washed up on the beach. The baby whelk population is quickly controlled, however; they feed on one another right after being hatched.

I have often wondered why on a beach like this we never have seen a lobster shell. Not far out on the water two lobstermen were checking their traps; we could see dozens of their lobster buoys bobbing in the waves and glinting wetly in the sun. There still are a good many lobsters in Nantucket Sound, and every lobster molts frequently, especially during its earlier years when it outgrows its shell at a faster rate. A five-year-old lobster, weighing about a pound, will have dropped its outgrown shell as many as 25 times. Perhaps the discarded shell is too fragile and breaks up before it is washed ashore. Whatever the reason, we could see that there were plenty of lobsters out there; a lobsterman was tossing two undersize specimens back into the water. But no signs of lobster could be found along the beach.

Nor were there many signs of man. A rutted Jeep track ran straight along the beach, as far as the eye could see; we knew that it reached from the tip of Coatue off the harbor entrance to the tip of Nantucket out on Great Point ten miles away. There had once been a small settlement of houses, and even a restaurant, dance hall and a bathing beach establishment on this sandspit; but all of it was gone, no doubt torn down for the precious lumber. The beach was left to the gulls and the crabs, making it a much more attractive place for occasional visitors like us. Only a few houses, widely spaced along the little peninsula and used sporadically by fishermen and duck hunters, remained to spoil the clean, open sweep of the outer beach.

We climbed back onto the low ridge and found that we were at a good spot to cross back—a narrow slot where the scalloped inner beach swings in between Second and Third Point. Even this thin stretch of sand bloomed with flora. What looked like a dense hedge was actually a growth of red cedar trees that have adapted to Nantucket's fierce northerly winds by spreading and hugging the ground like bushes; as if still leaning away from the wind, most of them grow toward the southwest. At the edge of the outer beach was another tree, the groundsel, also growing in low clumps along the ground.

A small flock of birds took to the air at our approach. They were song sparrows, land birds that are not supposed to inhabit a barrier beach like this. Evidently the song sparrows did not know this, because they were busily feeding on the beach plum bushes and the bayberries. They were the only land birds we saw on Coatue; perhaps, like us, they came out here for lunch, returning to the island's moors before dark.

As we were crossing the ridge we noticed a phenomenon that fortunately was occurring farther down the outer beach where the peninsula was a lot wider. This was what is called a blowout. It can happen when a particularly strong storm uproots a section of beach grass; the loss of one clump can start it. The dense network of plants that has anchored the sand is suddenly endangered. Their roots are exposed and the plants wither. More wind gets in under more roots. The gulf widens, the sand blows, and the dune starts to move. At a narrow point in the ridge a blowout could presumably result in a breakthrough. In 1896 and in 1933 a thin corridor of dune and grass at the head of the harbor, called the "haulover" because fishermen used to drag their boats over it from the harbor to the ocean, was broken through by particularly severe storms. No doubt both breakthroughs started with a blowout of the beach grass. The blowout on Coatue was a small one, and probably would repair itself before the gap became wide enough and deep enough for the ocean to pour through. The dune might shift up or down the peninsula or even across it toward the harbor. But more beach grass would take hold, more sand would build up around it, more shrubs and hedges would join the matted ridge, and Coatue would be preserved.

It was a little after noon as we crossed the ridge, and it was well that we had shoes. Even in September the dunes can become too hot for bare feet. At the height of summer's heat the dune surface can reach temperatures up to 120° F. So at midday there was little activity on the ridge. But we knew that we were walking over a veritable village of creatures burrowed under the sandy surface, hiding out from the heat of the day and waiting until night. Among the beach pea vines we saw a circular hole in the sand. Too small for a land crab, it was probably the home of the wolf spider, one of Coatue's more fascinating fauna. The wolf spider indulges in a bit of role reversal; instead of spinning a web and waiting for its prey, the wolf spider goes out looking for its victims, mainly insects, and it has adapted for its hunting role by growing longer legs than most spiders. The male wolf spider does the hunting while the female spider spends most of the summer in her burrow bringing up her young. The male usually does not join her during the day, but only at night when he brings home the ant or the fly. In the heat of midday he often hides out under a leaf near the burrow, but we decided not to poke about under the leaves looking for him.

We were across the ridge now, and before slithering down the far dune onto the inner beach we paused to enjoy the view: a graceful, sweeping vista, with gently swooping coves doing parabolas up the beach to the head of the harbor. The tidal currents were running faster, and we could see the currents and eddies across the sand bars that projected into the harbor to form each cove. Every curving beach was a perfect semicircle. A light breeze blew from the west, and wavelets lapped against the western sides of the sandbars while the water in the lee was a broad mirror.

We walked along the semicircular beach between Sec-

ond and Third Points, wading out into the calm, cool
water to look at the life on the bottom along the water's
edge. Not far from the low-tide line the water turned
darker; under it were acres of eelgrass, swinging slowly
in the current. The still, nourishing water of a bay or
harbor like this is sometimes referred to by zoologists as
the "primordial soup," whence everyone originated.
And this clear broth provided the home and nutriments
for millions of creatures, mostly small and some micro-
scopic. The eelgrass sheltered hundreds of varieties of
harbor life. Along its edges we were fascinated by one
species of inhabitant, the scallop. This attractive crusta-
cean, whose shell design is perhaps the best-known of
all, feeds on the rich plankton floating amidst the eelgrass. The scallops we found had ventured out and were
swimming about in the lee of one of the sandbars.

Swimming is scarcely the word; the scallops were actually jetting about, flapping their shells open and shut and
dashing along the bottom or zooming toward the surface
at amazing speeds. We could not have caught one with
our hands if we had tried—and it was just as well, I
learned from Dorothy Sterling's book: a pair of closing
scallop shells can snap off your fingertip.

Scallops are a proliferating species. There were hundreds in the one spot we were watching. Few seafoods
are more popular than the Nantucket Bay Scallop, and
these scallops seemed to assure at least a moderate supply for the next season, which would come in a month.
The water was alive with them.

I could only wonder how many scallops there must
have been a hundred years ago, because at that time the
scallop was not harvested; it was thought to be poison-

ous, perhaps because of the vivid colors of the animal within the shell. Even today it is only the scallop's muscle that you are served in a restaurant, and there are fishermen who claim to have seen cats that lost their tails after eating the rest of a scallop. All of the Nantucket Bay Scallop's meat, I am reliably informed, is safe and good-tasting.

I don't know whether the same is true of the sea scallop, or the deep-sea scallop as it is sometimes called. These larger cousins of the bay scallop are dredged up in deep-water areas like the Georges Banks, and only their muscles are served as food.

The muscle, by the way, is often incorrectly called the scallop's eye. In fact, the scallop has thirty to forty eyes. Moreover, they are bright blue. They are on the tentacles that fringe the scallop's mantle, and each eye has a lens, a cornea and a retina. Whether because of its excellent eyesight or a chemical ability to sense it in the water, the scallop can readily detect the approach of a predatory skate or starfish, whereupon it can shoot away with blinding speed—blinding to a starfish, but only marvelous to us. Evidently not realizing that we could be predators too (perhaps they knew the season wasn't open yet), these scallops were putting on a veritable ballet for us.

Even before predatory man comes out in October with his scallop rakes, there is vast mortality among these little crustaceans despite their evasive tactics. The inner beach in some areas was virtually carpeted with the distinctive shells. Studying one, we could detect the growth lines, ridges that form in the spring when the scallop renews its growth process after a winter's hibernation.

The only shells that competed with the scallops in

numbers, as we walked along the beach, were those of the slipper snail, or as some call it because of the slot that looks like a thwart, the boat shell. On some parts of the beach we found three or four of these little shells stuck to one another. And often we found a single shell still stuck to a rock or a clamshell. The young slipper shell moves about independently only until it is about half grown. Then it finds a likely looking surface—a rock or a discarded shell or even a still-occupied shell—and settles down for life. Cementing itself to this surface, it remains there. Often other slipper shells join the first one, cementing themselves one on top of the other until as many as a dozen are stacked up on the original surface. The still-connected groups we saw had died in tandem, so to speak, and drifted together onto the beach.

Other shells along the inner beach were far from dead. Hundreds of snails sat in the sand awaiting the incoming tide, the opercula of their shells closed tight, not so much because of our presence as to keep a bit of water inside the shell so the snail would not dry out between tides. Similar-looking shells got up and moved down to meet the rising water; these were hermit crabs, unfortunate creatures that do not grow their own shells and must find others in which to take shelter. The hermit crab carries its shell about with it, and has to discard it and find a larger one as it grows. The result is that the hermit crab, for all its clownish appearance, is an understandably mean-spirited creature. In a pool in the lee of Third Point we found a couple dozen hermit crabs. Some were chasing each other; two of them were fighting over an abandoned shell; and one was clearly trying to drag another out of a shell that was already its home.

It was in the perfect bay between Third Point and Five-fingered Point that we saw a slightly larger species of crab. Between the high- and low-tide lines a fiddler crab marched out and confronted our toes, waving its fighting claw in the air. The fiddler crab is so named because its left claw is large and its right claw small, and as the crab scuttles across the sand, the motion of the claws is much like the movement of a bow across a violin. Actually it is a fighting stance, with the large claw extended for action. But this particular crab evidently decided that discretion was called for, because it retreated in the direction of the water, still making threatening gestures in case we might mistake its retreat for weakness.

Along the high-tide line there was evidence that at first I took to indicate that some other crabs had had less fortunate encounters: carapaces of various shapes and sizes decorated the line of seaweed and other detritus. But these were not so much the remains of crab confrontations as cast-off shells. Like lobsters, nearly all crabs molt. When the crab's body becomes too large, the shell splits along the back, widening until the crab gently backs out. It leaves the shell behind and hides until a new shell hardens.

The blue crab is the best-known, of course, because it is marketed as soft-shell crab while it is between molt and its new shell. In fact, a crab fisherman can tell when a blue crab is ready to molt: when he sees the telltale line around the rim of the crab's shell, he puts the crab in a pool until it has backed out of its shell. Then, before it grows a new one, he sells it as a soft-shell crab.

The male blue crab, it happens, does what he can to

protect the molting female, partly because molting time is mating time. When the male detects the signs of molting in the female, he goes into a courting dance. As soon as the female has backed out of her shell, he covers her and implants his seed. He continues to cover and shield her until her shell has hardened. Then he leaves her to nourish her thousands of impregnated eggs. The female blue crab carries the eggs in her abdomen, finally depositing them on a sandy bottom of the bay just before they are ready to hatch. Then the process is repeated, the thousands of blue crabs backing out of their shells as they outgrow them, and leaving them to wash up and decorate the beach we were visiting.

We rounded Five-fingered Point (where did it get that name? I could not find out), and could see our boat, already afloat but secured by the stake I had driven into the sand above the tide line. On the edge of the sandspit was another candidate for the fireplace, a salt-whitened piece of driftwood that I detoured to pick up and carry to the boat. This piece of driftwood turned out to be interesting in itself: it was a victim of the shipworm, and one end of the log resembled a honeycomb more than a piece of wood.

The shipworm is not a worm but a mollusk. It descends on a piling or planking in droves, whereupon its shells actually change shape, becoming sharp, serrated blades. With these blades it bores a tunnel into the wood, swallowing the sawdust as it digs and expelling the waste through a siphon that it disgorges to trail behind it. This tube extends as the shipworm bores deeper, and the siphon ingests water and other nutrients at the edge of the tunnel; the tunnel may extend only an inch or so into the wood, but so many shipworms are at work at the same time that a piling can be riddled with holes and disintegrate in a few months. Since this process takes place underwater, the piling or plank breaks through and floats on the surface. When each tunnel is exposed to the air the shipworm dies; but by that time the thousands of shipworms in one log have released millions of offspring to attack other logs.

The one I found showed clearly how much of it had been in the water. Above the high-tide mark there were no holes. Below it there were a few, and they increased below that until the piling became a honeycomb and ended in a broken shaft of wood. No sign remained of the shipworms that had done their work and disintegrated; only the riddled wood testified to the months of boring by these termites of the sea.

I added this relic to the driftwood in the boat, brought our cooler up to the beach above the rim of seaweed indicating the high-tide mark, and we settled down for a late lunch of shrimp and Chardonnay. As we ate, some of Coatue's fauna proceeded to entertain us.

A row of gulls sat on the sandspit reaching into the harbor at Bass Point. The tide was rushing up the harbor now, and as the waves flowed over the end of the sandbar, one gull after another, its feet wet by the rising water, flapped its wings, rose, wheeled over the other gulls and settled at the dry end of the line, all in perfect order.

There was a flicker on the sand near us, and we realized that we had sat near a seaside grasshopper without even noticing it, so well camouflaged is this little insect. With the sun warming the sand, the grasshopper leaped up and fluttered through the air; when it landed it seemed to rise again, this time simply extending its legs to keep as far above the hot sand as it could.

There was another flurry of activity back of us, at the edge of the beach and the sea grass. In a little depression in the sand a couple of tiny creatures struggled for a moment; then all was still. From Dorothy Sterling's book I learned what had happened. The little cone-shaped sandhole was the home—and the trap—of an ant lion. The ant lion digs this tiny crater, using its head as a shovel, then hides at the bottom and waits for an unsuspecting insect to blunder into the hole. As the victim tumbles over the edge and struggles to climb back, the ant lion nips out and grabs its prey in its sharp pincer jaws, then burrows back under the sand to await its next meal.

The high point of our visit to Coatue came just as we were about to wade out to the boat. Along the water's edge came one of my favorite sea creatures, the horseshoe crab.

I have known and admired the horseshoe crab for most of my life. That is a long time, but an infinitesimal flicker in the time of the horseshoe crab. Its contemporaries were the ichthyosaurs and the dinosaurs of 200 million years ago, when Nantucket and a good part of America were deep under the sea. The other creatures of that time have been extinct for millions of years, but not the horseshoe crab. Through geological and climate changes on earth that have forced nearly every other living thing to evolve into vastly different beings, the horseshoe crab has gone on nearly unchanged. It looks and acts like the most impractical creature. Yet here, after 200 million years, was one pushing its way along the inner beach of Coatue.

It is not a crab but a relative of the spider. It has survived only on the eastern coast of the U.S.; a different species, indistinguishable to me, can be found in Asian waters. It is sometimes called the king crab. But its more popular name, horseshoe crab, is obvious from its outline. Its more or less streamlined, armored shape has evidently protected it through the millions of years. Certainly it does not seem an efficient organism. It moves slowly and laboriously. It has great difficulty righting itself if overturned on land; its long notched tail helps it turn over, but only after great effort. When approached by man, it is both defenseless and unable to flee, and uncounted horseshoe crabs are mutilated and killed by children who cannot resist grabbing the trailing tail. It propagates under the most difficult circumstances; and it is vulnerable when it is young and every time it molts.

Yet it survives, and has outlived all of its contemporaries. One reason is that the horseshoe crab is better engineered than it looks. Its combination of vision and eons-old instinct serve it well. The horseshoe crab has two sets of eyes, a large pair of compound eyes atop the center part of its shell and a smaller pair near the back. When the horseshoe crab is dug into the sand and nearly hidden, its forward eyes can still see. And even when it cannot see the water, it can almost always sense the right direction. Since it will sometimes become disoriented on a cloudy day, scientists guess that the horseshoe crab may get its sense of direction from the sun and the sky as birds evidently do.

I inspected this horseshoe crab by gently turning it

over, knowing that it should never be lifted by its tail. The five pairs of legs and single pair of pincers waggled in unison. The horseshoe crab has no teeth. As it pushes through the sand, the legs seize its food and pass it forward to its mouth, guiding the food on the way with the spines on its legs—like chewing with your hands. Near the base of the crab's tail its gill books—so-called because of their resemblance to the leaves of a book— waved back and forth; there are hundreds of them, and the horseshoe crab breathes through them.

On this bright afternoon my horseshoe crab was poking along the shoreline dredging up whatever grubs, roe, dead fish and other sustenance it encountered. But what I'd like to see—and never have—is its transformation at night. Then the plodding horseshoe crab slides out into deeper water, rolls over and, using its legs and gill books like oars, gaily swims about upside-down, evidently just for the fun of it.

Horseshoe crabs are a constant attraction to children, not only because of their curious prehistoric shape but also because of their interesting mating habits. "Double deckers," as our children used to call them when they found pairs of horseshoe crabs locked to each other in tandem and scrambling along our sea wall or crawling up onto the beach. Every May, at the time of the spring tide, the female horseshoe crab, with a smaller male clinging to her, searches out a sandy beach and trundles up just above the high-tide line. There she digs a shallow depression in the sand and lays her eggs. The male fertilizes them. Both return separately to the sea.

Beneath the thin layer of sand the sun warms the horseshoe crab eggs. For two weeks the high tide stops just below the eggs. But then the next spring tide washes over them and uncovers them. The eggs hatch and the baby horseshoe crabs are washed into the sea with the retreating tide.

They are nickel-size, nearly transparent miniatures of their parents. They ride about in the tidal currents and burrow into the wet sand. Fish gobble them by the thousands, and gulls feed on them when they come out of the water. Those that escape the fish and the birds outgrow their tiny shells and molt. They do not grow fast; at three years a horseshoe crab is only three inches wide. But gradually the survivors grow darker, tougher shells.

I recall the relief with which I discovered that the hundreds of dead horseshoe crabs I had found over the years were not fatalities but cast-off shells. A slit forms along the front edge of the shell; when it widens sufficiently, the horseshoe crab slips out of the forward part of the shell—instead of backing out as real crabs do. The shell floats to the beach and becomes part of the collection that my wife tells me I must soon dispose of before they fill our garage.

As the horseshoe crab grows and develops harder armor, it goes into deeper water. Slipper snails and barnacles cement themselves to the black shell; flatworms latch onto the horseshoe crab's underside. The mature crabs come ashore, in the spring for mating and in the summer to lumber along the shoreline like the one we found prowling Coatue's inner beach.

Turning my horseshoe crab right-side up, I watched it skitter into deeper water. It was also time for us to leave Coatue's beach. The outboard motor gratifyingly started again, and we raced across the harbor toward Pocomo.

At full tide the barrier beach behind us seemed a sliver of land, with the ocean surging against it on one side and the harbor tides swirling in circles along the other. On its narrow, gently rolling dunes the spreading hedges, trees and grass, warm and beckoning in the afternoon sun, were like a miniature of the Nantucket that for four centuries has been a lodestar in the lonely sea.

INDEX